"I suspect only a few of us have used the ph[...] it makes perfect sense, doesn't it? Reading well together [...] practice that can deepen our discipleship and bless the world. As Chris Smith convincingly shows, reading widely not only expands our personal horizons but enables us to serve our neighborhoods and bring renewal to the culture in ways that only bookish people can. *Reading for the Common Good* invites us into this holy adventure with the printed page—and what an adventure it will be! Put this book about books on the top of your list."

Byron Borger, Hearts & Minds Books

"In an era of partisan soundbites and Facebook memes, C. Christopher Smith's invitation to intentional, communal reading is a balm to the harried soul. With wisdom and compassion, *Reading for the Common Good* envisions reading and dialogue as disciplines toward cultivating and transforming communities, 'an essential part of a journey into a knowledge that is rooted in love.' I recommend this book to all who care about making disciples of all nations—one page and person at a time."

Tania Runyan, poet, author of *How to Read a Poem* and *How to Write a Poem*

"Chris Smith doesn't only demonstrate how books build communities, he shows how reading can be a virtue. In its diagnoses, social ecology and ability to make an impact on private and public life, this might just be the *Habits of the Heart* for a new generation."

Jon M. Sweeney, author of *The Enthusiast*

"In a world of constant noise and chatter, slowing down to listen as faith communities becomes a subversive act. In this great new book, Chris Smith invites us to truly listen to wisdom and stories shared through the written page. I highly recommend it."

Tim Soerens, cofounding director, The Parish Collective, coauthor of *The New Parish*

"Opening up *Reading for the Common Good* is like sitting down for a chat with the best kind of friend. C. Christopher Smith's references will provide layers of meaning and inspiration while his heartening and hopeful words will expand your soul."

Carol Howard Merritt, columnist, *The Christian Century*, author of *Healing Spiritual Wounds*

"Reading isn't a technique. It's about cultivating the practice of discernment through dialogue with others. I urge you to read this little volume if you are, like me, hungry for direction in a world that continually claims to know the right answers and the right techniques. To be still with others, to wait in reading 'texts' is an invitation to hear God together."

Alan Roxburgh, The Missional Network, author of *Structured for Mission*

"Let this book stoke the flames for rich communal life by doing something strange in our society: teaching us to read together. Chris sets a different pace with *Reading for the Common Good*, a pace that allows for a new flourishing in your neighborhood and mine by, yes, reading together! I couldn't be more taken by a book."

David Fitch, BR Lindner Chair of Evangelical Theology, Northern Seminary, author of *Prodigal Christianity*

"There are many books on the common good, but C. Christopher Smith's new book on reading for the common good is one of the most intriguing and compelling to come out in a long time. *Reading for the Common Good* weaves personal enrichment, ethics and education into a beautiful and simple unity. It is a paradigm-altering book and one that is sure to enrich and inspire as we seek to find meaningful ways to think about and engage our communities, cities and the world."

Ken Wytsma, author of *Pursuing Justice* and *The Grand Paradox*

"C. Christopher Smith offers a fresh, rich and quite unfamiliar proposal concerning human renewal and church regeneration. He exposits the cruciality of reading, thinking and conversing in the community as a bedrock practice for a sustainable missional community. His project serves to awaken us from our numbing 'electronic slumbers' into a slow engagement with imaginative words. I suggest that this book can be a valuable reference for pastoral nurture and education in the church."

Walter Brueggemann, Columbia Theological Seminary

"In this hectic age, with its flood of electronic scraps aimed at five-second attention spans, how refreshing it is to meet a champion of slow, sustained and meditative reading of books. And not just any books, but ones that nurture compassion and community. Chris Smith illustrates in his own work and in his account of the work of his church what it means to love one's neighbor. It means more than kindly feelings. It means kindly actions. It means caring for others, beginning with those who share the place where we live, and above all those who are most in need. The wealth Smith celebrates is not to be found in stock markets or bank accounts, but between the covers of books, between person and person, and in the loving heart."

Scott Russell Sanders, author of *Divine Animal*

"Having devoted the entirety of my personal and professional life to the vision and practices laid out in *Reading for the Common Good*, I offer a hearty 'Hear! Hear!' This book will inspire, motivate and challenge anyone who cares a whit about the written word, the world of ideas, the shape of our communities and the life of the church."

Karen Swallow Prior, author of *Booked* and *Fierce Convictions*

READING FOR THE COMMON GOOD

How Books Help Our Churches and Neighborhoods Flourish

C. CHRISTOPHER SMITH

Foreword by **SCOT McKNIGHT**

IVP Books

An imprint of InterVarsity Press
Downers Grove, Illinois

InterVarsity Press
P.O. Box 1400, Downers Grove, IL 60515-1426
ivpress.com
email@ivpress.com

InterVarsity Press® is the book-publishing division of InterVarsity Christian Fellowship/USA®, a movement of students and faculty active on campus at hundreds of universities, colleges and schools of nursing in the United States of America, and a member movement of the International Fellowship of Evangelical Students. For information about local and regional activities, visit intervarsity.org.

Scripture quotations, unless otherwise noted, are from the New Revised Standard Version of the Bible, copyright 1989 by the Division of Christian Education of the National Council of the Churches of Christ in the USA. Used by permission. All rights reserved.

While any stories in this book are true, some names and identifying information may have been changed to protect the privacy of individuals.

Cover design: David Fassett
Interior design: Beth McGill
Images: wall of open books: Vivien Leung / EyeEm/Getty images
abstract landscape: CSA-Printstock/iStockphoto

ISBN 978-0-8308-4449-4 (print)
ISBN 978-0-8308-9967-8 (digital)

Printed in the United States of America ♾

Library of Congress Cataloging-in-Publication Data

Names: Smith, C. Christopher, author.
Title: Reading for the common good : how books help our churches and neighborhoods flourish / C. Christopher Smith.
Description: Downers Grove : InterVarsity, 2016. | Includes bibliographical references.
Identifiers: LCCN 2016010691 (print) | LCCN 2016011226 (ebook) | ISBN 9780830844494 (pbk. : alk. paper) | ISBN 9780830899678 (eBook)
Subjects: LCSH: Church. | Christian life. | Christians--Books and reading. | Christians--Learning and scholarship.
Classification: LCC BV600.3 .S64 2016 (print) | LCC BV600.3 (ebook) | DDC 253/.7—dc23
LC record available at http://lccn.loc.gov/2016010691

P 20 19 18 17 16 15 14 13 12 11 10 9 8 7 6 5 4 3 2 1

Y 33 32 31 30 29 28 27 26 25 24 23 22 21 20 19 18 17 16

To my parents,

who taught me to read and to love reading;

and

to Englewood Christian Church,

who taught me to read for the common good

Contents

Foreword

Scot McKnight

At a recent party in a friend's home, a home we call Crick-hollow, a bundle of folks from Church of the Redeemer engaged in what we do at parties: casual conversations, and not a few of them invoking books and authors. At one moment Katie stood up to cite something from *The Lord of the Rings* and was answered by Dana and then Alex. A few moments later Marilynne Robinson's trilogy of novels—*Gilead, Home, Lila*—were extolled along with a few comments about whether it was better to have chapters or not. Dawne registered with us that she had not yet read any of them and asked which to read first, which led to a general consensus that *Home* is best. Kris and I agreed that was where to begin. Another conversation with Mike, Arnie, Kris, Alex and me was about theistic evolution, BioLogos, the so-called Cambrian explosion, Francis Collins and Michael Behe—and though there were some disagreements, there was a generosity of spirit and goodwill between all of us about all these topics.

Katie, one of our dear friends at Church of the Redeemer, somehow managed to break me of the habit of avoiding fiction by singing the praises of *The Lord of the Rings* two years ago and so I grabbed the three volumes, set them up on the shelf next to our bed and began to read them. I got through one and a half volumes before I wore down, but I did discover a good expression for a sermon at our church, and Katie smiled real big when I mentioned Tolkien. Kris's reading of *Gilead* provoked me to read it again, and then I was charmed enough to read *Home* while I was on sabbatical and was mesmerized by Glory and Jack and it led to one conversation after another with Kris and others at our church. We both read *Lila* and are now hoping Marilynne Robinson will write another, and at the party Kris said she hopes the next one will be about Glory's life or even Jack's. And once or twice I mentioned Robinson's novels in sermons, and others were drawn into conversation with me about how much they love her books.

We have two scientists—one a professor and another a medical doctor—in our church, so all conversations about evolution and Adam and Eve and the genome are ratcheted up to a level of intelligence that we theologians need to hear. (And we think they need to listen to us.) The topic, so it seems to me, is not best addressed in sermons or even adult Bible classes, but science and faith makes for a wonderful evening of discussion. I've learned and been pushed most about science and faith through conversations with other Christians.

Our church is a reading community. I don't know that the church has ever read one book in common, though our adult Sunday School class, COR@9, at times reads a book in common. Some of our small groups read books together as well. Others are drawn by relationships into coreading and endless conversations and allusions to what we have read. Our two preaching pastors—Jay and Amanda—are deep readers and quote from a colorful variety of authors, and not a few times I've chased down the books each has mentioned in sermons.

We are a different community because of Henri Nouwen, Eugene Peterson, C. S. Lewis, J. R. R. Tolkien and Marilynne Robinson. One of my own books, *A Fellowship of Differents*, has an illustration about a salad bowl (the original title, not liked by my editor, was *Life in a Salad Bowl*), and I first told that story in a sermon at Church of the Redeemer—and once a month someone at the church says something about our own "salad bowl." Church of the Redeemer finds some of its deepest diversity in the diversity of our reading and conversations.

Our unity at Church of the Redeemer is of the Spirit and in Christ through the Father's deep grace, but at work in that unity is a fellowship of shared ideas and beliefs and associations and joys and images and metaphors because we read similar books and talk about them with one another.

Chris Smith's book is a lovely adventure into a church's shared reading experiences, experiences that deepen fellowship but generate new paths of learning and growth. Not all Christians are readers, of course, and so one ought not to think that the only true churches are those that are also reading communities. But good church readers can learn how to communicate the best ideas of books being read and draw the nonreaders into the fellowship formed by the readers.

Perhaps what struck me most about Chris's book and his church were the books they were reading that Church of the Redeemer doesn't read, or at least hasn't. But that's how churches that read work: one person discovers joy in a book and passes that on, and that person then shares back another adventure in a book—and she tells a friend and a cycle of conversation about books starts. Others join in and before long the fellowship in Christ is tighter and deeper. For those who are readers it is nothing less than a great joy that the Lord of our faith is called the Word of God.

Introduction

The Local Church as Learning Organization

At the heart of the learning organization is a shift of mind—from seeing ourselves as separate from the world to connected to the world. . . . A learning organization is a place where people are continually discovering how they create their reality. And how they can change it.

PETER SENGE

My alarm goes off. I roll out of bed, get dressed and go downstairs. I put the dog on her leash and head out the door for a morning walk. As we move slowly down the block, I begin to think about the ways in which our little urban neighborhood has changed in the twelve years that our family has lived here. Many houses, once abandoned, have been renovated and now have families living in them. The community garden at the end of the block has doubled in size and now includes a picnic shelter and a small nature playspace with trees, wildflowers and even a stream for kids to play in.

Behind the garden is the former Indianapolis Public School Number 3. Twelve years ago, it was in major disrepair with a leaky roof and was surrounded by a barbed-wire fence. Today the barbed wire is gone, and the building has been restored and converted into thirty-two gorgeous, high-ceilinged units of mixed-income housing. The gymnasium attached to the school has also been restored, and in addition to a new basketball court and fitness equipment on the main floor, its roof has been converted into a deck hockey rink that now hosts games almost every night of the week.

At the end of my block I pause and look out across Washington Street, the historic Old National Road. I see the beginning of a new construction project, which will soon be a housing development for low-income seniors, and also the first residential complex in the state of Indiana with net positive energy use (meaning that the building will generate more solar and geothermal energy than it consumes). Twelve years ago this parcel of land was home to an abandoned commercial laundry facility that had leached chemicals into the soil for decades, creating a massive brownfield that had to be remediated, at a cost of well over a million dollars, before the present construction could begin.

I turn right and walk along Washington Street, passing the new Puerto Rican coffee shop that is only weeks away from opening and the tiny Mexican carry-out that has grown and thrived over the last three years since it opened. I see the murals, designed by my friend Brent, that not only add color to our neighborhood but also tell the story of the former amusement park that was built here over a century ago. I turn and walk past our church building, thinking about the ways that it has changed over the last decade: the addition of solar panels that provide 15 percent of the building's energy, the installation of an elevator that makes the full building accessible, and the development of an expanded, state-of-the-art daycare facility.

Working with our neighbors, our church has been deeply involved in all of these changes to our neighborhood. For many people, this story is hard to fathom, a *church* that is so deeply committed to—and engaged in so many ways in—the work of helping its neighborhood to flourish! Every couple of weeks or so representatives of another church or nonprofit come to visit us and to see what is going on in our neighborhood. Many of these groups want us to reveal a magic process or technique that will allow them to replicate these results back home. Although well-intentioned, these sorts of inquiries are complicated, and we rarely can answer them in a simple and straightforward way. Our aim, for instance, has never been to *do* all of these things. Rather our aim has been to immerse ourselves in the story of God's reconciling work. The primary work for us is not the redevelopment of our neighborhood but learning to submit ourselves to God's transforming work of renewing our minds and imaginations.

At a practical level, our church finds renewal in reading and having conversation with one another. Reading and discussing Scripture is primary as we seek to understand this story of God's creation and how it gives shape to our life together on the Near Eastside of Indianapolis. With the conviction, however, that God is reconciling all things "whether on earth or in heaven" (Colossians 1:20), we also find ourselves reading broadly as we seek to interpret Scripture and to embody Christ in our particular time and place: theology, history, urban theory, ecology, agriculture, poetry, child development, economics, fiction and more. Our emphasis on the virtues of reading broadly has led us to launch first a bookstore and later the *Englewood Review of Books*, an online and print publication that promotes the practice of reading in churches and recommends a broad range of books for its Christian audience.

As we seek to live faithfully in our neighborhood, we have come to understand that our life together is composed of two essential and interwoven threads: learning and action. On one hand our life together is marked by discipleship: learning to follow more deeply in the way of Jesus and to bear witness more fully to God's reconciliation of all things. On the other hand, we are engaged in a wide array of overlapping activities in our neighborhood: community development, economic development, early childhood education, gardening, alternative energy, caring for our neighbors (including ones that are often marginalized: the homeless, seniors, the mentally ill, etc.), publishing, extending hospitality, and many other types of work. Without learning, our action tends to be *reaction* and often is superficial—we act without comprehending the many factors that are at play in a situation. Without action, our faith is irrelevant, and most likely—to borrow a thought from the apostle James—dead. Although most churches tend to veer in one direction or the other, we need both learning and action in order to sustain healthy, flourishing communities.

Churches as Learning Organizations

Our experience at Englewood, as sketched above, resonates with business guru Peter Senge's depiction of a learning organization. In *The Fifth Discipline*, one of the bestselling business books of all time, Senge described the learning organization as one that is pursuing both learning and action, often woven together in a cycle of efforts to

• understand its context;

• imagine effective sorts of action;

• act and

• start the cycle again.

A learning organization, Senge observes, reflects the nature of our creation as human beings. First, we have been created to learn; we are inquisitive beings who long to know and be known.

"[Deep] down, we are all learners," Senge observes. "No one has to teach an infant to learn. In fact, no one has to teach infants anything. They are intrinsically inquisitive, masterful learners who learn to walk, speak, and pretty much run their households all on their own. Learning organizations are possible because not only is it our nature to learn but we love to learn."[1] "Real learning," Senge says, "gets to the heart of what it means to be human. . . . Through learning, we extend our capacity to create, to be part of the generative process of life. There is within each of us a deep hunger for this type of learning."[2]

Second, we have been created to live and work in community. When we see ourselves primarily as individuals, we often run the risk of working at cross-purposes with the organizations to which we belong. According to Senge, a learning organization is one that fosters *team* learning: "the process of aligning and developing the capacity of a team to create the results its members truly desire."[3] This requires the development of a shared vision, in which team members submit and interweave their personal hopes and dreams into a cohesive vision for the organization. However, it also requires a high degree of what Senge calls "personal mastery," which could be translated as a desire to excel at our personal vocations within the shared vision of the local church community.

In this book, we will view the local church as a sort of learning organization, in which both learning and action lie at the heart of its identity. We will explore the practice of reading—perhaps the most important component of learning in the twenty-first century—and consider how we can read together in ways that drive us deeper into action.

To imagine a church as a learning organization will require a dramatic shift in our understanding of the nature of church. Church can no longer be simply an experience to be passively consumed; rather, we are called into the participatory life of a community. Reading is a vital practice for helping our churches navigate this shift.

Members of a learning organization, as Peter Senge implies in the epigraph above, are coming to understand their power to create their reality.[4] Reading plunges us into the interconnected reality of creation, showing us our connectedness to people in other places and other times, reminding us how words on paper have the capacity to give shape to our everyday lives. Through language we are continually creating and refining reality. In our churches, we have the privilege of doing so together in ways that are attentive to the compassion, the justice, the healing and all the fullness of Christ. Our calling as God's people is to be a community shaped by this incarnational sort of learning. This is the very heart of discipleship, the way God has chosen to bear witness to the healing and reconciling of all creation.

THE COMPASSIONATE WAY OF JESUS

Jesus came into our broken, suffering world, embodying the way of compassion. The Latin roots of the word *compassion* mean "suffering with." Jesus suffered with those around him, and he calls us to do the same. Following Jesus in the way of compassion means entering into the pains and struggles of our churches, our families and our neighborhoods. Reading plays a role in a number of ways:

- forming us into the compassionate and faithful people of God, deeply engaged members of our church, our neighborhood and the world

- calling us to understand who God is and how God is at work in the world (particularly by reading Scripture)

- guiding us into a deeper understanding of our broken world and teaching us to imagine how such brokenness might begin to be undone

- discerning and developing our vocation—that is, how each of us might make our unique gifts available for God's healing and restoring work in the world

Reading carefully and attentively is an essential part of a journey into knowledge that is rooted in love. "[A] knowledge that springs from love," notes Parker Palmer, "will implicate us in the web of life; it will wrap the knower and the known in compassion, in a bond of awesome responsibility as well as transforming joy; it will call us to involvement, mutuality, accountability."[5]

As we hear the call of Jesus to follow in the way of compassion, we often experience a reflex that says *Just do something.* To ignore this reflex is to be hardhearted. But completely abandoning ourselves to it can also be less than compassionate; we can become so focused on "doing something" that we lose sight of those who are suffering. The way of compassion inevitably leads us into action. But we must be attentive not only to *what* is to be done but also to *how* and *why* the work gets done.

Our call to follow Jesus in the way of compassion is further complicated by the fact that injustice is not simply a problem to be fixed "out there." Injustice, or the desires that are the seeds of injustice, lives in all our hearts. Thomas Merton once issued an eloquent call: "[Instead] of hating the people you think are warmakers, hate the appetites and the disorder in your own soul, which are the causes of war. If you love peace, then hate injustice, hate tyranny, hate greed—but hate these things *in yourself,* not in another."[6] God is not only healing and transforming "other people," the ones whose brokenness seems more apparent than our own; God is at work in each of us, guiding us toward deeper faithfulness in the Jesus Way. The work of reading carefully and

well is one way in which God reveals to us a wider spectrum of
the desires of our hearts: those that point us toward the kingdom
of God and those that orient us toward evil.

READING AND DISCERNING TOGETHER

Although we are often inclined to think of reading as an individual
practice, and although most of our reading will inevitably be done
alone, the social way of reading that I envision here is guided by
choosing books and other reading materials that are intimately
tied to our communities—especially our church communities.
We all are called to follow in the compassionate way of Jesus, and
central to that calling is the work of carefully reading and medi-
tating on the scriptural story to understand who Jesus is. Not
everyone likes to read—indeed, not everyone *can* read—but a
vital part of our work as the church is equipping everyone to read
to the best of their capability and to participate as fully as possible
in our shared work of discerning the shape of our shared life.

This emphasis on the local church stems from a conviction
that the people of God are essential to what God is doing in the
world. God's work throughout history has been centered on
gathering a people who bear witness to a different sort of life
together. This work began with the Israelite people, the descen-
dants of Abraham, Isaac and Jacob.[7] When Jesus began his ministry, the community of apostles he called were the primary
people with whom he worked and shared life. After Pentecost
the wall of ethnicity was torn down, and Gentiles as well as Jews
were welcomed into the people of God. Our local church communities stand within this Pentecost tradition: we are local
manifestations of God's people in our particular places.

The primary work of the local church is discerning how we are
to live together in ways that embody the good news of Christ
among our neighbors. This process of discernment is largely

conversational; we come to know one another and how we fit together as we make decisions together. Reading is a crucial part of the process of discerning the shape of our life together. We read the Bible together, as well as other books that guide us to a deeper understanding of Scripture, books that help us better understand the times and places in which we live, and books that help us mature in our personal vocations within the church community. At Englewood we have benefited from reading broadly, but a caution is in order: although I think that reading broadly is healthy for churches, I don't recommend that every member of a church read broadly. Rather, I think that our personal reading will tend to focus on the areas of our gifts, passions and vocations, and when we read in this way, the reading of any church—taken collectively—will encompass a broad range of literature.

Reading is a vital practice that can—if done carefully and well—ultimately contribute to the health and flourishing of our communities. The term *flourishing* comes from roots that mean "flower"; to flourish is to bloom, to emerge into the full glory for which God has created us. Flourishing is the opposite of sin and brokenness and suffering. It is an English synonym for the Hebrew word *shalom*, which means total peace, health and well-being. Thus in these pages we will explore the sort of reading that moves us toward flourishing in our churches, our neighborhoods and the world at large.

I hope and pray that this book will serve as a sort of wake-up call—a call not only to deeper engagement and compassion but also to be increasingly aware of how God is working in and around us. I hope this book inspires us to imagine ways of deepening our shared life together. And I hope to make clear that reading is integral to all facets of our calling in Christ. May we all stay awake and grow in our awareness that in Christ "there is a new creation" (2 Corinthians 5:17) emerging from within our deeply broken and hurting world.

one

Slow Reading in Accelerating Times

Slowness means discovery. . . . [What] we get from even
a single good book, slowly and carefully read, is an education.
Moving at a deliberate pace, we discover what writers really
think, and as a result we develop our own minds.

DAVID MIKICS

I have always loved reading. My mom jokes that many of my childhood playthings are in pristine condition because I always preferred books to toys. Through my school years and into college, I read comfortably, not too slow and not too fast. (I did devour novels, but only because I was dying to know how they would end!) My reading habits changed drastically when I got into grad school, though. As a philosophy student whose schoolwork consisted primarily of reading and writing, I had to learn to speed-read just to stay afloat. It was not unusual to be assigned hundreds of pages of reading each week—per class! And it wasn't light reading either. On top of this, I was immersed in research projects that meant tackling stacks of books at once in order to understand their basic arguments and to hone in on specific passages that were relevant to my topic.

These new reading habits were only reinforced by my Internet activity. As part of the first generation to be fully immersed in Internet culture, I learned to skim and read at lightning speed, sorting through a deluge of information unleashed through email, websites, newsgroups and, more recently, social media. The Internet was a sprawling library that was always open. The same skills that enabled me to sort speedily through a stack of philosophy texts were further exercised online. I eliminated irrelevant messages, skimmed others and identified the ones most relevant to my interests at that moment. Grad school and the Internet changed the way I read. My default reading speed now is fast.

My experience is by no means unique. Research indicates that reading has not been killed off by the Internet. In fact, we now seem to be reading more than ever. But the way we read has shifted dramatically. We read faster. We prefer shorter pieces like blog posts and social media updates. The Internet presents us with billions of choices, all available at the click of a mouse, a few keystrokes or the swipe of a touchscreen. Social critic Walter Kirn has dubbed this "the nightmare of infinite connectivity." In a 2007 article for the *Atlantic* on how "multitasking is dumbing us down," Kirn says that corporations like Microsoft and Google proudly predicted that a world of limitless options meant freedom.[1] But the opposite has turned out to be true: without limits, we found not freedom but captivity.

One of the effects of this captivity is a condition psychologists call continuous partial attention (CPA). CPA is not the same as multitasking. When we multitask, we do one thing that requires most of our attention and other things that require less attention. (Multitasking might be writing while also listening to music and eating a snack.) But with CPA we are always on high alert, anxious about the possibility of missing an opportunity. This anxiety can be hazardous to our health. Linda Stone, the researcher who gave CPA its name, has said, "[Many] of us feel the 'shadow side' of CPA— over-stimulation and lack of fulfillment."[2]

CPA compels us to read frenetically. Studies indicate that people read webpages in an "F-pattern": starting with the headline and first couple of sentences all the way across the page, then scrolling down and picking out choice bits, our eyes never quite making it all the way to the right. Eventually we even tire of that, and our eyes follow the left margin as we scroll through the end of the article, completing the F. We may read more than ever before, but in the age of CPA few of us are reading well. We struggle to remember what we read or where we read it. "We have lost sight of the fact that reading requires time and patience," says literature professor David Mikics. "We must work hard to get more out of the books we read—and good books always reward slow-moving, careful attention."[3]

THE EMERGENCE OF SLOW READING

Just as eating is more than the consumption of calories and nu-trients, reading is more than mere consumption of words and ideas. As Thomas Merton put it, reading "is a deeply vital act not only of our intelligence, but of our whole personality, absorbed and refreshed in thought, meditation, prayer, or even in the con-templation of God."[4] Given the need that many of us feel for more substantial ways of reading, it comes as no surprise that in recent years there has been a growing call for a Slow Reading movement.

To understand the scope and promise of a Slow Reading movement, we need to put it in context with other interrelated "Slow" movements that have emerged in recent years, as more and more people desire to resist the demands of a sped-up tech-nological age. The Slow Food movement came first. Launched in Italy in the late 1980s as a reaction against fast food, fast life and the homogenizing forces of globalization, Slow Food promotes buying and eating local food, cooking it yourself and lingering around the table with family, friends or neighbors. Following in the footsteps of Slow Food came other Slow movements: Slow Cities, Slow Parenting, Slow Money and Slow Fashion. What these movements all have in common is not just the *means* of acting slowly and attentively. They also share a common *end*: the cultivation of local community. Slow Food, for instance, celebrates not only the community of eaters sharing food but also the community that is forged as food buyers and food producers come together in thriving local food economies.

The Slow movements offer a way of living and being that stands in contrast to the speed and fragmentation of mainstream culture—what sociologist George Ritzer referred to as the "McDonaldization of society."[5] The Canadian journalist Carl Honoré helpfully summarizes the differences between *fast* and *slow* in his book *In Praise of Slowness*: "Fast is busy, controlling, aggressive, hurried, analytical, stressed, superficial, impatient, active, quantity-over-quality. Slow is the opposite: calm, careful, receptive, still, intuitive, unhurried, patient, reflective, quality-over-quantity. It is about making real and meaningful connections—with people, culture, work, food, everything."[6]

Although Slow Reading is still relatively young as a movement, David Mikics, author of *Slow Reading in a Hurried Age*, has suggested that it has a long prehistory. He traces the origins of the term to Reuben Brower, who taught a course with this name at Harvard University in the 1950s. The history of the practice, however, he traces back much further, to the midrash of ancient Israel. As Jewish rabbis sought to understand and interpret Scripture, they developed habits of inquisitive and conversational engagement with the biblical text that they called midrash.

After centuries of midrash, centuries spent in conversation not only with Scripture but also with other strands of the midrash tradition, many of these conversations became codified in the Talmud. What's striking about this practice of slow and careful reading is that it was not just practiced by scattered individuals but rather was rooted in the common life of a particular community.

Mikics's vision of Slow Reading emphasizes the mechanics and benefits of reading a book slowly, being attentive to all the dynamics that unfold in the intersection of author, reader and text. But even though Mikics offers these valuable historical insights, and even though he is attentive to the social dynamics between author and reader, one of the shortfalls of his work is that it does not offer a robust vision of how Slow Reading—like Slow Food, Slow Church and other Slow movements—has the power to transform communities.

Mikics's shortcoming, however, is the strength of Isabel Hofmeyr's account of Slow Reading in her book *Gandhi's Printing Press: Experiments in Slow Reading*. Hofmeyr describes how slow, intentional reading helped transform a particular historical community—the community of expatriate Indians in South Africa in the early twentieth century. Natives of India were first brought to South Africa as slaves in the late 1600s. South Africa outlawed slavery in 1838, but the number of working-class Indians grew, though they faced intense discrimination.

One vital force that helped unite the Indian community in South Africa was the International Printing Press (IPP), cofounded by Mohandas Gandhi. Hofmeyr argues that the IPP provided an important tool with which Gandhi could experiment with forming the identity of his community. Gandhi used the IPP to cultivate practices of slow and attentive reading that shaped the identity of the expat Indian community in South Africa.

Reading bound them to each other and helped them live well in a country that was not their homeland.

Reading attentively in our church communities, as citizens of another kingdom exiled in our particular nations and neighborhoods, will draw us closer to one another and deeper into the life of our places.

SLOW READING IN OUR CHURCH COMMUNITIES

Although Slow Reading is a fairly young movement, the Christian tradition—building upon the reading and conversational practices of the Israelite people—has a long and rich history of reading slowly and carefully. In her bestselling memoir *The Cloister Walk*, writer Kathleen Norris describes how in the fall of 1991 she settled in for a prolonged stay at St. John's Monastery in rural Minnesota. During her time at the monastery, she was profoundly shaped by the monks' practice of lectio divina, the monastic way of slowly reading, praying and reflecting on Scripture. Lectio divina, Norris came to realize, is not a process of dissecting the texts, rendering them devoid of life, but rather a kind of listening that brings life and flourishing to both the text and its hearers.

The history of lectio divina can be traced back at least as far as St. Benedict in the early sixth century.[7] The Rule of St. Benedict describes and orders the life of the monastery. It is a deep well of wisdom from which monastic communities have drawn over the last millennium and a half, as they have sought to be flourishing communities of Jesus' disciples. Benedict names two essential practices with which the monks should occupy their days: manual labor and lectio divina. These activities are prescribed as means of avoiding the trap of idleness, "the soul's enemy." Although Benedict's recommendations vary with the seasons, he generally recommends that the monks spend three hours each day in lectio divina, and on Sundays as much time as possible.

The monks of Benedict's time and later centuries devoted much of their lives to lectio divina because they understood this practice as a school in which we not only hear Christ, the Word of God, but also learn what it means to devote our whole selves to following Christ as part of the people of God. Christians of our own day often lose sight of the reality that our call to be disciples of Jesus means that we are to be students: hearing, studying and, most importantly, following in the way of Jesus. "In any master-disciple relationship," writes noted Benedictine monk and author Michael Casey, "the content of what is learned is less important than the relationship itself; it is prolonged mutual presence that communicates to the disciples the spirit and the style of the elder. Lectio divina helps us to encounter Christ, it initiates us into the way of Christ."[8]

The monastic tradition of lectio divina also reminds us that our call to discipleship always unfolds in community. Even prior to St. Benedict, *lectio divina* was a term used to describe liturgical readings in the church congregation and was thus a practice undertaken in community. In Benedict's day, and for centuries afterward, lectio was practiced in the monastery, a particular community in which the Word of God was heard, discerned and embodied. Lectio divina, which guides us into a deeper faithfulness to Jesus, must also lead us into a deeper life together in our local churches and with Christian sisters and brothers from around the globe.

THE PRACTICE OF LECTIO DIVINA TODAY

As it developed into a rich monastic practice over the centuries, lectio divina came to be defined by four elements: reading (*lectio*), meditation (*meditatio*), prayer (*oratio*) and contemplation (*contemplatio*). Just like the elements in a chemical compound, the elements of lectio divina are intermeshed with one another and cannot easily be isolated. It is possible to separate them from each other, but that would require significant effort, and the resulting elements would be substantially different from the original compound.

Although lectio divina is a sort of dance, the four elemental practices circling around each other, the process of reading the text (*lectio*) is primarily a linear and orderly activity. Although we may read the text with our eyes, the intent of *lectio* is to hear the text, and particularly the text as it was originally spoken: the psalms, for instance, as they were chanted aloud by the Israelite people, or Paul's epistles as they were read aloud in the church at Corinth or the churches of Galatia.

To the monks of Benedict's day and throughout most of the Middle Ages, silent reading was scarcely known; almost all reading was done aloud. Through vocal reading, the body was trained as well as the mind. In contrast, we in the twenty-first century prefer the written word to the spoken one, as it is easier to control. Although reading is a crucial practice—as I am arguing in this book—we need to be ever aware of its limitations. Eugene Peterson offers this warning: "But *caveat lector* [reader beware]: we do not read the Bible in order to reduce our lives to what is convenient to us or manageable by us. . . . Writing is derivative of speaking. And if we are to get the full force of the word, God's word, we need to recover its atmosphere of spokenness."[9]

The aim of the *lectio* step is not analysis, breaking the text down and interrogating it, but simply listening to it as it flows off of our lips in one slow, steady, continuous stream. Questions will inevitably arise as we listen to the text, but *lectio* is not concerned with wrestling with them, only perhaps "jotting them down" in the back of our mind for further scrutiny later.

If *lectio* is the process of reading and listening to the text, *meditatio* is a conversation with the text. We pull out some of the images and memories that we encountered in *lectio* and begin to turn them over in our mind or to develop them on paper. Sorting through these thoughts is itself part of *meditatio*, as we decide which are worth exploring further. The task of *meditatio* is to reflect on the meaning of the text in its original context, as well as how that meaning might translate to churches in our day. Imagination is crucial. We consider the world in which the biblical texts were written and what they might have meant there; we further consider what the text might mean in today's world and how the two very different worlds are connected. For instance, what did Jesus' parables mean to his disciples and others who heard them, and how might that meaning translate to our time and place?

In *oratio* (prayer), the third elemental practice of lectio divina, we encounter God in the text. Prayer is fundamentally about entering the presence of God. Just as Moses was transformed when he encountered God firsthand on Mount Sinai, so too we cannot help but be transformed as we abide prayerfully in the presence of God. The spirit of prayer is one of submission, perhaps best depicted in Jesus' prayer in the Garden of Gethsemane: "Not my will, but yours be done" (Matthew 26:39). Prayer pervades the whole process of lectio divina, as we enter all four of the elemental practices with expectant hearts, desiring to encounter and abide in the presence of God. "[Prayer] accompanies us as we open the book and settle our mind, as we read the page and ponder its meaning," observes Michael Casey. "Prayer is the meaning of lectio divina."[10]

Although prayer is ultimately about submitting to the will of God, our posture should not always be one of passive submission. The psalms, long recognized as the prayer book of God's people, reflect a wide range of emotions as their writers encounter God. We have been created with emotions and desires, and we bring them with us as we encounter God in the text through lectio divina. *Oratio* is the conversation that ensues as we bring our desires and emotions about the text into God's presence, and it reminds us that we do not read alone; we encounter God in the text. "Without prayer," writes Michael Casey, "*lectio* is less *divina*; it becomes mere reading."[11]

The fourth and final elemental practice of lectio divina is *contemplatio*, in which we begin to imagine how the text is to be lived out within our everyday life. Just as we encounter God in the text through *oratio*, in contemplation we encounter those whose lives are intertwined with our own: the brothers and sisters of our church, our family, neighbors, coworkers and so on. This understanding flies in the face of the usual ways we think about contemplation: that is, as a practice disconnected from everyday life, done by nuns and monks in monasteries. The wise Benedictine David Steindl-Rast wrote: "Contemplation joins vision and action. It puts the vision into action. Action without vision is action running in circles, mere activism. Vision without action is barren vision."[12] Contemplation is thus the bridge between our hearing of the text and our beginning to act upon it. In the next chapter we will explore in detail the social imagination that shapes our sensibilities of what is possible and the ways in which reading forms this imagination. Contemplation is the arena in which our social imagination takes shape and is continually re-formed.

In the four interwoven elements of lectio divina we have inherited from our Christian ancestors a powerful way of Slow Reading. While we never should cease reading Scripture in this manner, this way of reading, encountering God and imagining new social realities can also happen with texts *beyond* the Bible.

Preaching as Slow Reading

There is another familiar practice of Slow Reading that we have inherited in the Christian tradition: preaching. At its best, preaching is focused on understanding and embodying the biblical text; it requires a listening and engaged congregation. If a sermon is merely a religious product to be consumed and eventually disposed of, then there is little hope of transformation and flourishing. Preaching is a corporate act of reading Scripture together. Cornelius Plantinga has described preaching as "the presentation of God's word at a particular time to a particular people by someone the church has authorized to do it."[13] In this definition we see that although one person may be standing up and doing the preaching, the two most important components of preaching are the church—who authorized the preacher and who hears the text—and the text itself.

In order to explore preaching as a type of Slow Reading, let's examine one of the most famous literary sermons—preached by Father Mapple in Herman Melville's classic novel *Moby-Dick*—through the lens of the four elemental practices of lectio divina described above.

Father Mapple's sermon, preached in the whalemen's chapel in New Bedford, occurs early in the novel, before Ishmael, Ahab and others set sail on the *Pequod*. The biblical text for the sermon is the book of Jonah, but especially the last verse of chapter 1: "And God had prepared a great fish to swallow up Jonah." Given the relevance of this passage to the storyline of the novel, the sermon is generally understood as foreshadowing the whaling adventures that will follow.

Prayer. Prayer is closely coupled with preaching. Like many preachers, Father Mapple prefaces his sermon with prayer. He also closes the sermon by gesturing a prayer of benediction. These "prayer bookends" suggest that *oratio* is most importantly practiced in how a congregation—both preacher and laity—prepares to encounter God in the biblical text of the sermon. Melville doesn't tell us much about the congregation that gathered in the chapel on the Sunday of Father Mapple's sermon, but there is no doubt that the minister had a deep understanding of his audience and their seafaring ways. The language and imagery of the sermon show that he was prepared to narrate Scripture in language that would connect powerfully with its hearers.

Although Melville doesn't tell us much about Father Mapple's congregation, the laypeople's preparation to encounter God is no less significant than the preparation of the preacher. In his classic work *Celebration of Discipline*, Richard Foster emphasizes that an essential part of worship is a people who gather with "holy expectancy," ready to encounter God in their midst. "The early Christians gathered with anticipation," he writes, "knowing that Christ was present among them and would teach them and touch them with his living power."[14] One important aspect of preparation is for each member of the congregation to approach the sermon with a humble spirit that is quick to listen and slow to become angry. All too often we are formed by the consumerism of our day to approach preaching with a "what's in it for me?" mentality. The sermon is a reading of the biblical text for the benefit of the whole church community, and we should prepare ourselves to be attentive for not only what we need to hear as individuals but also what the whole church needs to hear.

Reading. Following the common practice of many churches, Father Mapple reads his primary biblical text, Jonah 1:17, aloud at the outset of his sermon. Then he proceeds to narrate most of the book of Jonah in his own paraphrase that fits the context of the whalemen's chapel. In some church contexts the passage to be preached on will be read aloud earlier in the service. In other contexts the preacher will read the passage aloud verse by verse in the course of the sermon. Either way, the act of reading Scripture aloud is a type of *lectio*. The congregation hears the text. If we are attentive and the text is read slowly and well, we abide with the text, parts of it will stick with us, and questions about it will arise in our minds.

Meditation. The bulk of Father Mapple's sermon is focused on the tasks of meditation and contemplation. He helps his congregation reflect on the meaning of the Jonah story both in its original context and in today's world (*meditatio*) and inspires their imaginations with thoughts of how they can embody the meaning of the passage in all the particularities of their time and place (*contemplatio*).

Exegesis is an essential part of meditation, exploring the language and culture in and around the passage in order to shed light on what it might have meant for those to whom it was originally written. Father Mapple, for instance, spends a good chunk of his sermon explaining the geography and economics of Jonah's day by comparing ancient places to modern ones that would be familiar to his seafaring listeners. The whole Jonah story, as it rolls off Mapple's tongue, is saturated with nineteenth-century sailing terms that would resonate with those who wandered into that seaside chapel. Father Mapple's comparisons of Jonah to the apostle Paul remind us that exploration of how a text fits into the larger witness of Scripture as a whole is another important task that fits within the scope of meditation.

Contemplation. With pointed exhortations like "Sin not; but if you do, take heed to repent of it like Jonah," Father Mapple challenges his congregation to *contemplate* the meaning of Jonah's story for their own lives. Although most sermons today similarly call us to imagine a way forward from the text into action, contemplation can be enriched in the local church context by creating space for a broader conversation about how a sermon's text might be embodied. Although the preacher does play a vital role in leading the church, the task of discerning and embodying Christ ultimately falls to the congregation as a whole. All too often in our culture of pervasive individualism, members of the church are left to apply and embody the text as they see fit (or not) in their personal lives. Perhaps the contemplative element of the sermons in our churches is not as robust as it could be, but there is in fact almost always a contemplative call to imagine how the text might be embodied.

Lectio, meditatio, oratio and *contemplatio* are all present in some form or another in Father Mapple's sermon and most others. Indeed, as a form of lectio divina, preaching is a way of Slow Reading. Preaching and lectio divina remind us that Slow Reading is not unknown to the church today. But in order for these practices to slow us down and offer a way of living and being that stands in contrast to the speed and inattentiveness of the broader Western culture, we need to find ways to do this sort of reading intentionally and mindfully.

One substantial barrier to a careful and attentive practice of Slow Reading is that all too often we understand reading as a personal practice and have little or no sense of how reading not only transforms the way we see and experience the world but also transforms the ways in which our communities operate. As we seek to remove this barrier, the next chapter will highlight the *social imagination*—that is, the accumulation of shared stories and categories through which our communities make sense of the world—and how reading is absolutely essential to the forming and re-forming of the social imagination in the modern world. And, of course, as our social imagination is transformed, we find that our living and acting within our world will likewise begin to take new and deeper forms.

two
.....

Shaping the Social Imagination

There is no Frigate like a Book
To take us Lands away
Nor any Coursers like a Page
Of prancing Poetry—
This Traverse may the poorest take
Without oppress of Toll—
How frugal is the Chariot
That bears a Human soul.

EMILY DICKINSON

I was about eight years old when I first read Madeleine L'Engle's Newbery Award–winning novel *A Wrinkle in Time*. L'Engle's suggestion that our world might consist of more than three dimensions captured my imagination. Since then I have been fascinated by the ways in which we imagine and talk about the spaces we inhabit. Years later I would be introduced by one of my college professors to a book that explores similar themes, Edwin Abbot's nineteenth-century novel *Flatland*.

Flatland is the story of A. Square, an actual square who lives in a two-dimensional world. The first half of the novel is a description of the culture of Flatland—a thinly veiled satire of Victorian society. The second half of the novel is more relevant today. It recounts A. Square's adventures in both lower dimensions (Lineland) and higher dimensions (Spaceland). In Lineland, A. Square tries and ultimately fails to describe Flatland to the king. The king lacks the experience and language needed to imagine the possibility of a two-dimensional world. Later, A. Square is transported from Flatland to Spaceland by a visiting sphere, who reveals to him the mysteries of that three-dimensional world. When he returns home, A. Square tries in vain to tell others about what he saw in the higher dimensions. For this he is imprisoned. He eventually realizes the futility of these efforts, and instead he transcribes his story in the hope that "these memoirs . . . may stir up a race of rebels who shall refuse to be confined to limited dimensionality."[1]

Our experience of life is shaped by our social imagination: the collective ordering of reality through experience, language and culture. We draw upon the social imagination as we consider future possibilities as a society. *Flatland* is fascinating to me as a clear, if somewhat simplistic, illustration of how the social imagination works. A. Square's experience of three-dimensional Spaceland had little or no transforming power in his own day because Flatlanders didn't have the capacity to imagine the possibility of a world beyond their own. (Similarly, the king of Lineland was unable to imagine the possibility of Flatland.)

Just as the society of Flatland is ordered by their experience of reality—the physical properties of their bodies, the values they attribute to various persons, the built environment in which they live and so forth—so our society is shaped by our experience of the world and our capacity to articulate and imagine new possibilities. Although we undoubtedly have unique experiences as individuals, it is not the individual experience that is the primary force in the ordering of reality but rather the collective experience of the communities in which we live. It is our churches, neighborhoods, work communities, nation-states and transnational cultures (such as Western culture) that ultimately provide the shared language and experience with the power to order daily life. Returning to the example of *Flatland*, we notice that A. Square's personal experience of Spaceland, and his capacity for articulating that experience, was not sufficient to transform the social imagination of Flatland.

How then is our social imagination transformed? The seeds of transformation lie, I believe, in a community (or subcommunity) that has an alternate vision of how life could be structured. Scripture repeatedly emphasizes that God's people are to be a contrast society.[2]

In the Old Testament, Israel is frequently reminded of its call to be a holy people, a community set apart for the purpose of demonstrating a different, contrasting way. Similarly, the New Testament writers speak of the kingdom of God in contrast to the world. For instance, "if anyone is in Christ," writes the apostle Paul, "there is a new creation: everything old has passed away; see, everything has become new!" (2 Corinthians 5:17). We live in the world and have been formed by the world, and yet at the same time God is at work forming us in a way that bears witness to the kingdom of God. In his book *The Prophetic Imagination*, Walter Brueggemann emphasizes that we have been called as the people of God "to nurture, nourish, and evoke a consciousness and perception alternative to the consciousness and perception of the dominant culture around us."[3]

In order for us to imagine ways of reading that lead us deeper into the flourishing that God intends for the world—the primary task of this book as a whole—this chapter begins by establishing a basic understanding of the social imagination: what it is, how it is shaped and transformed, and how it shapes us.

THE SHAPE OF OUR LIVES

Drawing on the work of a number of contemporary social philosophers, I use the term *social imagination* here in a broad manner, incorporating all the ways in which we talk about, understand and order our everyday experience. We often make decisions in our daily lives without much reflection. Even when we do carefully reflect before making a decision, our options are usually limited to a small set of choices. The social imagination is the force at work shaping reality behind and throughout our decision making. One of the ways in which the social imagination functions is by narrowing options—sometimes to the point that our action can happen without much reflection at all.

On a map, my finger can trace a multitude of routes between two points, say my house and the grocery store. However, if I am actually trying to go to the grocery store, there are significantly fewer possible routes due to the way land has been divided up. In a car that presumably will stay on roads, there may be only a couple of reasonable routes.

Roads, fences, property lines and all the structures that give shape to our life are contained within the social imagination. The theories that lie behind these structures—theories of human development, scientific theories, our theology, and so on—and even the language we use to articulate those structures and theories, are also part of our social imagination.[4] These structures include, but are not limited to, the following:

- The structure of language: We speak in and write in English with the Roman alphabet and Arabic numerals.

- The structure of time: Our calendar is divided into 365 days, our weeks into 7 days, our days into 24 hours, and so on.

- The structure of our education: Children in our culture generally start schooling in kindergarten at about age five. They study for thirteen years before entering the workforce or going to college.

- The structure of our economy: One dollar will buy *this* amount of food (or other goods). That same dollar represents *this* amount of work or other resources.

- The structure of the built environment: Roads, sidewalks, medians, fences, buildings and alleys are all structures that give shape to our lives and experience.

The structures of all facets of life are contained within the social imagination: at home, at work or at church—even the structure that inclines us to think of these three as distinct spheres of life. Our churches have structures that are contained within the social imagination. What days of the week do we gather? What do we do when we are together? How do various people in the congregation function within the gathering—for example, pastors, musicians, children? How do we celebrate important holidays? Do we follow the liturgical calendar? Do we celebrate the Eucharist or Mass or Communion? If so, how often, and what are the traditions and policies that govern how we do so?

Sometimes structures remain long after the undergirding theories have lost legitimacy. Some churches today, for instance, forbid women from preaching on the basis of passages like 1 Corinthians 14:34: "Women should be silent in the churches." Historical research has shown that in first-century churches such as the one at Corinth, where women were largely uneducated, Paul's instruction was aimed at maintaining order in the church service.[5] In that context, women regularly asking questions of their husbands during the church service would have been rather disruptive. In North America today, however, where women generally have the same educational opportunities as men, the theory and practices that led to the apostle Paul's instruction no longer hold. And yet some churches still maintain structures that prohibit women from preaching.

The Social Imaginary

At the heart of what I am referring to as the *social imagination* lies what Canadian social philosopher Charles Taylor has called the *social imaginary*.[6] Taylor defines the social imaginary in this way:

> What I'm trying to get at with this term is something much broader and deeper than the intellectual schemes people may entertain when they think about social reality in a disengaged mode. I am thinking rather of the ways in which they imagine their social existence, how they fit together with others, how things go on between them and their fellows, the expectations which are normally met, and the deeper normative notions and images which underlie these expectations.[7]

Taylor offers two illustrations. The first is voting. There are all kinds of assumptions and background that give shape to our understanding of the election process. For instance, there are the convictions that underlie it: for example, that it includes "all citizens, choosing each individually, but from the same alternatives, and the compounding of these microchoices into one binding, collective decision."[8] Each facet of the process could be done differently, and indeed has been done differently in other nations, but there is a specific way in which we have come to imagine the election process in the United States.

Taylor's second example is the demonstration, which is also part of the social imaginary in modern democracies. We know the written and unwritten rules that define this ritual: citizens assembling, making and carrying banners, marching. Taylor describes the way in which we imagine what a demonstration is:

> The background understanding which makes this act possible for us is complex, but part of what makes sense of it is some picture of ourselves as speaking to others, to which we are related in a certain way—say, compatriots, or the human race. There is a speech act here, addresser and addressees, and some understanding of how they can stand in this relation to each other. There are public spaces; we are already in some kind of conversation with each other. . . . The mode of address says something about the footing we stand on with our addressees. The action is forceful; it is meant to impress, perhaps even to threaten certain consequences if our message is not heard. But it is also meant to persuade; it remains this side of violence. It figures the addressee as one who can be, must be, reasoned with.[9]

The social imaginary is a historical construct, built up over time, through language, experience and culture. "It can never be adequately expressed in the form of explicit doctrines," Taylor says, "because of its very unlimited and indefinite nature."[10] The social imaginary is therefore more than philosophy or theory; it is the complete accumulation of language and experience that gave shape to particular theories, as well as the unique ways in which particular theories—for example, Einstein's physics, Freud's psychology, Locke's political philosophy, free-market capitalism—are woven together to provide a common structure for our social life together, one that is always being negotiated and revised. In the early twenty-first century we live and function within multiple social imaginaries. There are the broad social imaginaries of Western culture and the Judeo-Christian tradition, which share a great deal of overlap. There also are more specific social imaginaries within each of these broader ones: for instance, we have the imaginary of Lutheranism within the Judeo-Christian tradition and the imaginary of the Evangelical Lutheran Church of America within that. Every community to which we belong has its own social imaginary located within a series of expanding imaginaries.

If I am a biochemist who works for a particular pharmaceutical company, I function not only within the social imaginary of the biochemistry profession but also within the social imaginary of that particular company, which is within that of the pharmaceutical industry as a whole, which is within the imaginary of free-market capitalism, which is within the imaginary of Western culture. We often learn to function within a particular social imaginary without actually accepting the convictions that give it its particular identity. I might work for a company, for example, without sharing all the convictions that shape how that company understands and operates within the world.

In an example that hits closer to home, many people who participate in our churches do so without sharing all the convictions central to our identity. In churches that officially adhere to biblical inerrancy, there are undoubtedly members who do not share this conviction. Similarly, in churches that affirm same-sex couples, there are people who maintain a traditional view of marriage.

These examples acknowledge the existence of individual imaginaries in addition to social imaginaries. As a result of Enlightenment philosophy, individualism is one of the prevailing powers in Western culture. We have been conditioned to think and act in isolation from others. Although I am focusing here on *social* imaginaries, I do recognize the impact that our individualism has on the social imaginaries of the groups to which we belong. Although a church, neighborhood or other local social group may have a particular way of thinking about, talking about and enacting a thing, there will inevitably be within that group a range of ways that individuals accept, reject and nuance social expectations. These individual ways of imagining the world will eventually have some bearing on the shape of social imaginaries, but they also often create dissonance and may at times serve to fragment social groups.

An important part of becoming a vital learning organization, Peter Senge observes, is allowing our individual imaginations and visions to contribute to the forming of a shared vision. He writes:

> Visions that are truly shared take time to emerge. They grow as a by-product of interactions of individual visions. Experience suggests that visions that are genuinely shared require ongoing conversation where individuals not only feel free to express their dreams, but learn how to listen to each other's dreams. Out of this listening, new insights into what is possible gradually emerge.[11]

Prior to the modern era, *local* social imaginaries had greater power to shape reality than they do today. Certainly there were some broader imaginaries at work in the premodern era—for example, Western culture, Roman Catholicism, Islam—but such things as language, time and economics were mostly defined by local culture. Many of the most powerful intermediary social imaginaries in today's world—nation-states, transnational corporations—did not exist in the premodern world, or they were distantly removed from day-to-day living.

The recent emergence of local food movements, "Buy Local" campaigns and other attempts to promote local culture can be seen as reactions against globalization and attempts to shift determinative power away from large-scale social imaginaries and back toward local ones. This shift is a beneficial one for our local church communities. It provides the opportunity for us to begin imagining the shape of a life together in Christ that stands in contrast to the ways of Western culture at large. While it is helpful for us to understand the broader social imaginaries within which we live and function, most of the emphasis in this book will be on a social imagination that is driven by local social imaginaries, especially those of church and neighborhood.

The emphasis on the local social imagination gives us leeway to consider and experiment with the ways in which social imaginaries are transformed. Walter Brueggemann suggests that the prophetic imagination, the imaginative work that leads us deeper into the flourishing that God intends for creation, is both *critical* of the dominant powers in the world and *energizing* by giving new life and energy to alternative ways of living and being. But as individuals and local communities, we have little power to influence the shape of broad social imaginaries like that of Western culture or that of the United States. These larger imaginaries have taken shape over centuries and have a sort of inertia that inhibits them from rapid change. With the rise of globalization and Internet culture, we may now be living in an age of rapid transformation of some of the larger social imaginaries—but such changes happen on the scale of decades or centuries, not days or even years.

It is much easier for us to comprehend how social imaginaries are transformed when we begin locally. Since the social imaginary encompasses language, theory and structures, a permanent shift in any of these facets yields a transformation of the social imaginary.

READING AND THE SOCIAL IMAGINATION

Reading, of course, will inevitably expand and transform our *individual* imaginations, but it also plays a crucial role in changing our *social* imaginaries. Through reading, we encounter new and different language, theory and structures. Although we also encounter these things in other forms of media, in reading we encounter them in deeper ways. Unlike broadcast media, reading permits us to control the pace at which we engage the content; unlike video, reading requires us to imagine the work in our heads. In other words, we cannot simply be passive consumers of what we read, even when we are reading primarily for amusement.

Of the three main genres that we will examine here—fiction, nonfiction and poetry—it's probably easiest to see how nonfiction affects our social imaginations. Within the broad genre of nonfiction, let us consider three distinct subgenres: narrative (biography, history, memoir), theory and instructive (the how-to book or article). Other than acknowledging its existence, I won't elaborate on *narrative nonfiction* because it functions in ways that are nearly identical to fiction. *Theory*, as noted above, is one of the elements of the social imaginary, and actively reading theory—for example, theology, philosophy, science, sociology, psychology or literary theory—will impact how we see the world. Of all the genres and subgenres examined in this chapter, theory is perhaps the most challenging to read. Yet because of its direct connection to our social imaginaries, it is beneficial for us to read at least a little theory from time to time.

One genre that often gets overlooked is *instructive nonfiction* (or, the how-to book), but such works do have an important role in how we structure and imagine the world. Doing a thing well— whether creating a permaculture garden, knitting a hat or fixing a car—is important to flourishing cultures. A particular social group will not value every practice, but it won't value *any* practice without at least some basic sense of how to do it.

Although its impact on the social imagination might not be as direct as that of the nonfiction genres considered above, fiction (and I would also include drama and narrative nonfiction in the same category) can play a powerful role in transforming the social imagination. Fiction gives us the capacity to try on other social imaginaries. "Reading is a technology for per-spective-taking," writes Steven Pinker.[12] Jane Austen's novels, for instance, allow us to insert ourselves into the social imaginaries of nineteenth-century England, just as reading *The Odyssey* or *The Iliad* permits us to imagine ourselves in ancient Greece.

In his provocative book *The Better Angels of Our Nature: Why Violence Has Declined*, Pinker not only makes the case that vio-lence is decreasing on planet Earth but also contends that this decrease can be attributed, at least in part, to the rise of the novel. "Realistic fiction . . . ," he writes, "may expand readers' circle of em-pathy by seducing them into thinking and feeling like people very different from themselves."[13] Noting that printing technology and the rise of the novel preceded the humanitarian revolution of the seventeenth century, he goes on to recount a long list of popular novels that "all raised public awareness of the suffering of people who might otherwise have been ignored."[14] This list includes Charles Dickens's *Oliver Twist* and Herman Melville's *White Jacket*, as well as more recent narratives like Elie Wiesel's *Night*, Alex Haley's *Roots* and Azar Nafisi's *Reading Lolita in Tehran*.

Sometimes, as in dystopian fiction like Aldous Huxley's *Brave New World* or Suzanne Collins's Hunger Games series, we insert ourselves into stories in cautionary ways; the story emphasizes for us particular language, theories and structures that are *not* bene-ficial to human health and flourishing. Other works of fiction may call into question the theories or language by which we imagine the world. For instance, Harriet Beecher Stowe's *Uncle Tom's Cabin* called into question the language, theories and structures related to the American antebellum practice of slavery. The transformative power of fiction comes to bear primarily on our language and structures and to a lesser extent on our theory. Douglas Coupland's novel *Generation X* not only gave a name to the post-boomer generation but also introduced a vast lexicon of other creative terms—highlighted and defined in the book's margins—that have embedded themselves in common usage, including "slumming" and "the veal fattening pen" (AKA cubicle). George Orwell's classic novel *1984* introduced and developed the familiar concept of "Big Brother," an authoritative power that is watching every move of its subjects. Science fiction novels like Madeleine L'Engle's space trilogy often help us imagine different structures through which our life could be ordered. Well-written historical novels, such as Shusaku Endo's *Silence*, immerse us in a particular situation and in so doing often unsettle some of our theories and structures and challenge us to imagine new ways of sharing life in our communities. Historical fiction also affords us the opportunity to examine historical events from multiple vantage points and with a deeper appreciation for the complexity of that historical moment. Geraldine Brooks's novel *Caleb's Crossing*, for instance, offers a profound and complicated account of the relationship between Puritans and Native Americans in seventeenth-century New England.

Poetry is, in essence, the art of noticing. Through a carefully crafted image, the poet reveals to us beauty that we might never have discovered for ourselves. "[Beauty] is so quietly woven through our ordinary days," wrote the late Irish poet John O'Donohue, "that we hardly notice it. Everywhere there is tenderness, care and kindness, there is beauty."[15] Poetry forces us to slow down and to devote our attention to beauty.

It tunes our aesthetic imagination, ever revealing to us that which is beautiful, and training us to imagine a future that is rooted in deeper sorts of beauty.

Poetry also influences our social imagination on the level of language. Some poems, like Robert Frost's "The Road Not Taken," introduce new idioms into our vocabulary—in Frost's case, "the road less traveled." Often, however, the function of poetry is not providing terms that will endure as part of the social imagination but simply articulating and helping us appreciate certain experiences in new and fresh ways. For instance, in the Emily Dickinson poem at the beginning of this chapter, the poet describes the book as an oceangoing vessel taking us on a voyage to other lands. Like fiction, a poem can craft an alternative world with its own social imagination—either in a few short lines, as William Carlos Williams did in his poem "The Red Wheelbarrow," or in a much longer work such as the epic poem *Beowulf*.

THE TRANSFORMATIVE POWER OF CONVERSATION

Reading is most socially transformative when paired with the practice of conversation. Our personal reading cannot transform social groups without some sort of conversation—written or oral, online or face to face—through which reading is shared, engaged and discerned.

For the last twenty years my church community, Englewood Christian Church, has gathered for conversation every Sunday night. The first few years of this conversation were spent refining the language (and the associated theology) that we used as evangelicals. We started with the question, What is the gospel? Eventually we moved on to other questions: What is the church? What is salvation? What is Scripture and how do we read it? What is the kingdom of God? In these early years of our conversation, as we refined our language and our theology, our local social imaginary was transformed in powerful ways, and we began to act in ways that reflected this shift.

My church's experience has shown us that, without a doubt, the most important factor in the transformation of local social imaginaries is conversation, both formal and informal. "In dialogue," writes Peter Senge, "a group explores complex difficult issues from many points of view. Individuals suspend their assumptions but they communicate their assumptions freely. The result is a free exploration that brings to the surface the full depth of people's experience and thought, and yet can move beyond individual views."[16] And "prophetic imagination as it is derived from Moses," writes Walter Brueggemann, "is concerned with matters political and social, but it is as intensely concerned with matters linguistic (how we say things) and epistemological (how we know what we know)."[17]

Conversation is the space in which all of these elements intersect: where language is refined, where we ask difficult questions of one another and where we become convinced of certain courses of action. Formal conversations that contribute in powerful ways to how we imagine the shape of our life together include decision-making conversations about governance and finance. Education is another formal conversation space because it is there that language is taught, and new or competing theories can be introduced.

Informal conversation also plays a vital role in transformation. As we talk about the shape of our life together, we articulate, often unintentionally, our imagination about how our social group should function. Around water coolers and dinner tables, we reveal and refine our beliefs about the structure of the world. We talk about the news, weather or the movies, and sometimes our opinions will differ. Although such conflicts might easily be brushed aside as trivial, they do occasionally lead us into deeper conversations about why we differ. These conversations may alter our shared language, theories or even practices over time. They may also at times lead to public forums or other types of formal conversations. Conversation is only one way that our local social imaginaries are transformed. Local change often occurs as a result of changes in the broader social imaginaries. Sometimes we simply adopt the changes of the larger culture. We regularly inherit and appropriate terms and phrases that are swirling around in our media-saturated culture. Terms like *AWOL* (inherited from the military), *stat* (from medicine) and *strike three* (from sports) are in common use today. Further, we regularly inherit theories and structures from the culture at large—though these may be a little trickier to identify.

The cultural shift over the course of the twentieth century from getting around on foot or by horse to getting around in petroleum-powered vehicles is a structure that most social groups—with the notable exception of the Amish—have accepted. Other times, shifts in broad social imaginaries are rejected or reacted against. The Amish rejection of not only petroleum-powered vehicles but also electrical technology is a pointed example. Perhaps more familiar is the rejection by most evangelical groups of the cultural shift to permit abortion on demand. The development of crisis pregnancy centers to offer alternatives to women who want to protect the lives of their unborn children arose largely as a response by those in the pro-life movement.

The practices of reading and conversation are vital for the process of transforming our social imagination. Part of the human experience is imagining how the world should function. The question is, what stories are feeding and shaping that imagination? Reading renews and energizes our social imagination. For our churches, reading and embodying Scripture is the foremost source of renewal, but renewal also comes from reading, reflecting on and discussing a broad range of works in light of the life and teaching of Jesus.[18] In the next six chapters we will look specifically at how reading is vital for fostering flourishing communities in the church, in the neighborhood and in the world at large.

three

Reading and Our Congregational Identity

What we study determines the kinds of habits that are formed, which is why Paul urges us to focus on things that are true, honorable, just, pure, lovely, and gracious.

RICHARD J. FOSTER

Our bodies are, to a large extent, an exhibition of the choices we have made, the gods we have served, the places we have lived, the work we do, our habits of eating and sleeping and playing. Some facets of this historical record are immediately obvious. I may, for instance, choose to trim or not trim my hair or my beard. Some people may have arthritis or other physical challenges as a result of repeating the same task over and over. On the other hand, a sedentary lifestyle also has its harmful effects on our bodies. Other characteristics of our bodies are the record not of our own personal choices but of those of generations of ancestors, now coded into our genes. Humanity adapts over many generations to patterns of climate, diet and work. Our complexion, hair color, muscular and skeletal structure are all products of the rich history of our ancestors, the places they have lived, their diets and many of their other habits.

EMBODYING JESUS

Although modern Christianity tends to elevate the spiritual realm over the material, our bodies play an important role in our faith. Incarnation matters to Christians. God takes on flesh in the person of Jesus. And we are called to *embody* Christ in our local church communities. Writing to the church at Corinth, the apostle Paul says: "You [plural] are the body of Christ and individually members of it" (1 Corinthians 12:27). Paul's language is important here. I don't embody Christ as an individual. The universal church as a whole also is not Christ's body (although there is a larger sense in which this is probably true). Rather, our local churches—including the one in first-century Corinth and the ones to which you and I belong—are manifestations of the body of Christ. Together, sisters and brothers in church communities in distinct local places give a particular body to Christ that our neighbors can see, interact with and experience. Undoubtedly the body of Christ taking form in my local church, and most other local churches, is broken, misshapen and immature—but we cannot forsake our calling to embody Christ together. To the extent that our church bodies are healthy and faithful, we will continue to mature over time toward "the full stature of Christ" (Ephesians 4:13).

Our church bodies, like our physical bodies, take the shape of the choices that we make together. We are called to embody Christ, but how do we grow in our understanding of who Christ is and what his mission is? And how do we make choices that lead us into deeper, more mature faithfulness in our embodiment of Christ? In short, we are a learning organization that is focused on reading and dialogue. Specifically, we read, reflect upon and discuss Scripture, which is the church's trusted account—passed down through the ages—of who Jesus is and what he is doing in the world. It is no coincidence that the apostle John refers to Jesus as "the Word"; there is a deep connection between Jesus and Scripture. Although the temptation to elevate the text of Scripture over Jesus is strong in some Christian circles, it is Jesus who is sovereign, the One who is the very heart and meaning not only of Scripture but of all creation. "Christ, the Incarnate Word," writes Thomas Merton, "is the Book of Life in Whom we read God."[1] Scripture shows us who Jesus is and thus also the nature and the character of the people we are learning to become.

In their important book *Reading in Communion*, Stephen Fowl and Gregory Jones make the case that "the vocation of Christians is to *embody* scripture."[2] Our primary calling is not merely to read or to analyze Scripture, they suggest, but to allow it to shape us into the image of Christ, the Word incarnate.

We are not just reading a dusty book of stories from many centuries ago; we are reading a story in which we are actors. In recent years some theologians have described the scriptural story as an improvisational drama. Actors in improv theater are given a basic plotline and instructed to work together to act it out. Scripture is the basic story we've been given, and God offers us immense freedom and abundant opportunities to bring it to life. Improv requires that actors be ever attentive to the plot that they have been given and to the time and place in which they are acting; when this work is done well, the actors will keep the audience engaged.[3]

Reading together is not necessarily the same as reading in communion. Many churches offer frequent opportunities for their members to read together—for example, Bible studies or book discussions—but not as many churches are interested in reading in communion. Reading in communion is reading that draws us into a deeper shared life with one another and with our neighbors. It is a formative practice that shapes our church communities into more integrated and more mature embodiments of Jesus. Unfortunately, reading in communion with the brothers and sisters of our local church community does not come naturally for us in West, formed as we have been by the individualism of the modern era. René Descartes, who lived and wrote in the mid-seventeenth century and is considered to be one of the forefathers of modernity, wanted to set aside everything that had gone before him and establish a system of knowledge based solely on his own experience. Since Descartes, individualism has rolled through history like a snowball, gradually picking up more speed and influence.

Individualism affects how we read Scripture, but reading in communion is one way to counteract the influence of individualism. For example, our individualistic ways of reading Scripture are exacerbated by the English language's failure to distinguish between the singular and the plural *you*. Almost by default then, we read many passages that were written in the second-person plural, including the above passage from 1 Corinthians 12, as if they are speaking to us individually. But when we read and embody Scripture together in a local church, we can benefit from the gifts of pastors, scholars and others with knowledge of the biblical languages. They can reveal the subtle grammatical choices of the biblical writers and help us unpack the implications.

That said, pastors and scholars can't do all the work for us. We all have to wrestle with Scripture as we seek to embody its story together. "No particular community of believers can be sure of what a faithful interpretation of Scripture will entail in any specific situation," Fowl and Jones emphasize, "until it actually engages in the hard process of conversation, argument, discussion, prayer and practice."[4]

How We Read in Communion

What are the dynamics of reading in communion, this conversational way of wrestling with and embodying Scripture? Fowl and Jones describe three intertwined dimensions of this process: reading the text, the text's reading of us, and our reading of the world.

We read the text. Of these three dimensions, the most familiar—and the one that we have focused on thus far in this chapter—is reading the text. God's people, as the scriptural story emphasizes, are called to be a holy people, a community whose way of life stands in contrast to that of the surrounding nations. It is by reading and submitting to Scripture that we are shaped into the holy people that God intends us to be. There is always a temptation to rely on "the wisdom of the age," and maybe especially so in the early twenty-first century, when Internet media are seemingly inescapable and partisan ideologies hold so much power over the public imagination. Reading and embodying Scripture together is what makes us the church; it distinguishes us from other social and economic groups. Scripture is not an arsenal we draw upon to defend our partisan politics. Rather, it is the light by which we are able to assess and engage ideologies of all sorts. Reading Scripture reminds us who we are as God's people and helps us clarify that identity within the ever-changing dynamics of our particular time and place.

The text reads us. Reading the text, however, is not enough. We must also allow the text to read us. In contrast to the academic biblical scholar (for whom the Bible might become simply another text to be analyzed), the church submits itself to Scripture and allows it to shape our life together. So in addition to interrogating Scripture, we must also allow ourselves to be interrogated by it. And in allowing it to ask questions of us, we allow it to shine the light of Christ on our lives and to guide us toward deeper faithfulness to the way of Christ.

How does such an interrogation happen? Fowl and Jones offer two examples. First, Scripture calls into question the baggage we all bring to our reading of it:

> [We] come to Scripture with particular predispositions, ideologies, and theological presumptions. Left unchallenged, we will fail to recognize the corrupting power of these predispositions, ideologies, and theological presumptions. The interrogative power of Scripture challenges us to be constantly reforming the preconceptions we inevitably bring to interpretation. For example, the biblical identification of "God is love" has yielded a popular picture in middle-class America that God is a "therapeutic nice-guy." This picture needs to be challenged by such texts as Amos where God demands repentance and justice rather than prescribes therapy.[5]

The second example they offer is our willingness (or lack thereof) to wrestle with difficult texts. Noting that the passages we find difficult might vary between cultural contexts (for example, the story of the rich young ruler is difficult for most North American Christians), we need to struggle with these passages that seem difficult or offensive to us and "not primarily suited to [our] own desires."[6] In affirming our commitment to grapple with Scripture, and to abide in these sorts of tensions, we allow it to read us, speaking into our lives and times.

We read the world. As Scripture reads us, it also helps us to read the world. Since God created all things and called the creation good, and since God is at work healing and reconciling a creation broken by sin, our call to bear witness to this reconciliation must necessarily unfold in the world. In order to faithfully embody Jesus in the world, we must seek to discern and depict the social, economic and political relations that constitute the world. Therefore we need to interpret carefully the contexts in which we find ourselves, and Scripture informs and directs our efforts to make sense of these contexts. Scripture, however, does not read the world apart from other human efforts to understand and articulate the world. Although Scripture is the primary narrative for God's people in the church, it reads the world in conversation with other texts and other voices, both inside the church and outside it.

In the mid-1980s my church made the decision to stay in our urban neighborhood and not to move out to the suburbs where many of our members were living at the time. This decision launched us into a journey of trying to understand what it meant for us to live faithfully in this place. We read scriptural passages like "Love your neighbor as yourself" and "Whoever has two coats must share with anyone who has none." These texts read us and convicted us that we weren't doing a very good job of knowing and loving one another, let alone our neighbors. We watched and talked with other urban churches and decided that we should start pantry ministries (food pantry, clothing pantry, furniture pantry, etc.).

As our church continued on our journey of seeking to be faithful in our place, we started to ask questions like "Why do many of our neighbors keep coming back to our pantry week after week?" In the light of Scripture, we grew in our awareness of the role of corporations, government, nonprofits and even churches as powers and principalities that propagate injustice in our neighborhood. This growing awareness led to reflection on how we were to relate to these powers, both struggling against them (Ephesians 6:12) and bearing witness to them (Ephesians 3:10).

Scripture, in conversation with the work of theologians like Marva Dawn and Walter Wink, was helping us to make sense of the complex dynamics at play in our neighborhood.

READING OTHER BOOKS IN COMMUNION

Scripture is our primary text. If God is reconciling *all* things in Christ, however, our churches should be engaged in a broad range of work that bears witness to the comprehensiveness of God's reconciliation. In doing so, we will read many texts that guide us into that work. Fowl and Jones offer a couple of examples to stir our imaginations:

> We need to consider, learn from, and also criticize sources and resources other than Scripture which address both the tasks of ethics and particular moral issues. For example, if we are addressing the problems of hunger in the world, we will need to draw upon the resources of economic analyses as well as international politics. Or if we are addressing issues of medicine, we will need to draw on the resources of contemporary scientific investigations.[7]

Furthermore, our reading should not be limited to instructive nonfiction. Literature that is done well, even popular fiction, often sheds *at least* as much light on ourselves and our world. Our reading should include fiction and poetry, and some members of our congregations will be more inclined to read these genres of books. In his book *The Love of Learning and the Desire for God*, Jean LeClercq emphasizes the vital role that reading classical literature of the Greeks and Romans had on the shape of monastic communities in the early Middle Ages. In addition to the practice of lectio divina—the slow, prayerful reading of Scripture described in chapter one—medieval monks read a broad range of classical works from Greek and Roman authors:

poetry, philosophy, drama, history, government and more. What did the monks inherit from these classics? LeClercq asks.

They took the best that these authors had to give. Through contact with [the classics], like all who study the humanities in any period, they developed and refined their own human faculties. To begin with, they owed to the classics a certain appreciation of the beautiful. . . . At times [the monks] drew moral lessons from these authors, but they were not, thanks be to God, reduced to looking to them for that. Their desire was for the joys of the spirit, and they neglected none that these authors had to offer. So, if they transcribed classical texts it is simply because they loved them. They loved the authors of the past, not simply because they belonged to the past but because they were beautiful with a beauty which defies time.[8]

LeClercq also notes that the medieval monastics read the classics with an eye to convert them—that is, when the monks encountered passages that were wise and relevant, these ideas were woven into their theology. The reading habits of medieval monks are instructive for us today because they were located within particular Christian communities and oriented toward the goal of those communities to embody Jesus together. Long before Peter Senge coined the term, medieval monasteries were learning organizations. Their reading was focused on prayerfully interpreting Scripture through lectio divina but was intermixed with diverse selections of classic works that resonated with the ideals of beauty and truth. In addition to prayer and manual labor, this practice of reading was one of the most formative habits in medieval monastic communities.

We would be wise to learn from these ancient monks in our readings today, seeking that which is true and beautiful and wise regardless of its origin and weaving it together with our ever-developing understanding of the scriptural story, as we seek to make sense of the world and to faithfully embody the cruciform way of Jesus within it.

One crucial arena in which reading is essential to the flourishing of our churches is identity.

THE IDENTITY OF OUR CHURCHES

As humans, we are continually on a journey of identity, a quest to understand who we are. This journey is not solely spiritual, or mental, but one that is deeply physical as well. As a manifestation of Christ's body in a particular place, each of our churches is on a similar journey. Scripture gives us many clues that point us in the direction of our identity: we are the embodiment of Jesus; we are the temple of the Holy Spirit; we are the salt of the earth; we are the light of the world. These biblical passages are familiar, but what do they *mean*? In the most concrete of terms: Who is this Jesus? What was he about? What story (or stories) gave meaning to his life and work? Who is this Holy Spirit of God who tabernacles in our midst (1 Corinthians 6:19), and what does that mean for how we share life with one another and with our neighbors?

As a body, we exist in time and space, within the particularities of history and a certain place. Our quest for identity cannot evade the questions: *Where* are we? What does it mean to exist within the human culture, the flora and fauna, the landscape, the topography, the climate, of this place? *When* are we? What are the spirits and the powers that define our age? How have we arrived at this particular stage of history?

This search for our identity is similar to what Fowl and Jones have called "Scripture reading us," but this process does not unfold in a vacuum. Although the primary actors in the scriptural story are God, the people of God and Scripture itself, there are a host of other actors and forces that also give shape to our identity. Our explorations in identity, although ever lit and guided by the light of Scripture, will involve engaging the world, starting with the particular corners of the world that are most intimate to us. Reading is vital to these explorations.

How do we undertake this journey together in our local churches? For clues, we once again look at our own physical bodies: how do all the parts of a body—brain, heart, limbs, all the way out to the tips of our extremities—collaborate to make sense of the world? It might sound a bit peculiar to describe it in this way, but the process is essentially a *conversation* between the brain and all the other parts of the body, a conversation that is carried on through the nervous system. Sensory data is passed from parts of the body to the brain, and the brain sends guidance to the parts of the body in response. The body parts respond in action; sometimes, if the action is difficult, the body parts might also respond with pain. And this cycle repeats itself again. Back and forth from the brain to organs and extremities, a bodily conversation unfolds.

Similarly, if our local church as a singular, unified body—the embodiment of Jesus—is seeking to understand and engage the world around us, we will need to be in conversation. It is not enough for each individual member to be reading and seeking, and for us to hope that we will somehow magically cohere into a singular body. It is also insufficient for the conversation to unfold solely among congregational leaders. How healthy would our bodies be if we completely ignored our hands and our fingers or our feet, legs and toes? No, everyone who God has gathered in our church community is a part of our body, and we need to find ways to make them active participants in the conversational work of understanding our identity.

Just as anatomy is integrally connected with physiology in our physical bodies, so identity is interwoven with vocation (the topic of the next chapter) in our churches. Who we are is bound up with the gifts and skills that God has provided in the members of our congregations, and in a spirit of gratitude, we need to be attentive to the gifts that God has lavished upon us in all of our church members. It is in conversation that we not only discover these gifts but also discover how they fit and work together as a body with a singular mission.

Unfortunately, conversation is not highly valued in twenty-first-century Western culture. As Bill Bishop has explained in his book *The Big Sort: Why the Clustering of Like-Minded America Is Tearing Us Apart*, we North Americans increasingly order our lives such that we are surrounded by people similar to ourselves. One of the effects of this is that we begin to lose the capacity to carry on civil conversation with those who differ from us, economically, racially, ethnically and so on. Public interactions in the twenty-first century tend to take the form of clashing ideologies instead of conversations that lead us toward collaboration and the common good. Indeed, our own churches rarely provide spaces for conversation that are open to the body as a whole. The challenge for churches today is either to create those spaces or to find ways to integrate the conversations that are already going on in smaller groups—Sunday school classes, small groups, Bible studies—into the conversational life of the body as a singular whole.

Conversation is the way in which we listen to Christ, our head, and discern together how to follow and enact his leading. Many churches bypass conversation with authoritarian leadership—but to do so is to substitute human leaders for Christ as the head of our body. I'm not saying that our churches shouldn't have leaders. Our physical bodies have organs that connect and energize the body as a whole (for example, heart, stomach, nervous system), but these organs are clearly not the head that is leading and guiding the body, and the organs do not function autonomously from the rest of the body; they must work in cooperation with the other parts.

Reading, as explored in this book, is essential to the health and flourishing of our churches. However, reading and conversation must go hand in hand. Reading that is most beneficial is reading that takes its cues from and is shared and discussed—in some way or another—with the local church body. Just as a body works together—seeing, feeling, listening—to understand its identity, so our churches are faced with the task of working together to understand our identity. Reading is a valuable tool in this process of discerning our identity, but only to the extent that it is shared and discussed for the benefit of the whole body.

Who and Why Are We?

Scripture, of course, is the primary story through which we come to understand who we are. However, reading an English translation of the Bible can present numerous challenges. The first challenge, as I have hinted at already, involves translation. What did the biblical texts mean in the languages in which they were originally written? We will need some people in our churches who have familiarity with Greek and Hebrew and can help us navigate the challenges of translation.

If we are to be the body of Christ, then we must explore vital questions about who Christ is. Reading works in biblical studies and theology—commentaries, studies of first-century culture, works of theology and church history—can shed some light on these questions, helping us understand what the biblical text meant in the language and culture in which it was written and how Scripture has been interpreted in other times and places. Understanding the scriptural story is essential to deepening our sense of identity as a local church body. All members of our body should have at least a basic understanding of biblical studies and theology and will occasionally read books or parts of books that continue to foster a deeper understanding. Some members, of course, will go much deeper than that and will guide the congregation toward deeper understanding of who Scripture calls us to be and of the ends toward which creation is moving.

Although works in biblical studies and theology are important tools in discerning our identity, they are not the only type of reading that will help us wrestle with the questions of who we are and why we are. Other nonfiction works will shed light on the human experience and in this way also play a role in helping us understand who we are.

• Philosophy asks a lot of difficult and probing questions about human experience. Alasdair Macintyre's *After Virtue* explores the significance of virtues, tradition and community, for instance; Michel Foucault's work explores the dynamics of power in the contemporary world.

• History, sociology and cultural studies can help us to understand better how our cultures have taken the form they have and can help us name the types of brokenness in and around us. The work of social critics like Neil Postman, who is best known for his critiques of technology (*Technopoly*) and media culture (*Amusing Ourselves to Death*), and Bill McKibben, best known for his critiques of ecological devastation (*Eaarth*), are especially important for us as followers of Christ who desire to embody an alternative to mainstream culture.

• Works in psychology, like Viktor Frankl's *Man's Search for Meaning* and, more recently, Susan Cain's *Quiet: The Power of Introverts in a World That Can't Stop Talking*, can also give us insights into what it means to be human.

Well-written fiction can do many of the same things as nonfiction, probing the human experience, but its use of story can grab our attention and challenge us to examine our condition in ways that nonfiction often fails to do. Poetry can provide new language or images that lend powerful insight into the human experience.

WHEN AND WHERE ARE WE?

Questions of *who we are* and *why we are* not the only ones that we need to consider. We also must wrestle with the questions of *when* and *where we are*. "Where are we?" is a question that is fundamental to our identity. It will be explored in more detail in chapter five, on flourishing neighborhoods. The challenge of understanding *when we are* involves discerning what it means to live in this particular age and how the present day is interrelated with previous ages. Reading history, of course, will be essential to understanding the times in which we live, but news and commentary will be equally important. Reading politics and economics also will help us understand our times.

Once again, contemporary poetry and fiction can shed needed light on the times in which we live, often helping us to see connections in ways that narrow, siloed genres of nonfiction—politics, economics and the like—cannot.

I should emphasize that we need to be ever attentive to *why* we are reading and not just *what* we are reading. Our end is not to make a successful life for ourselves and our family, or to navigate the turbulent waters of our times successfully. Rather, our end is to understand our times in order that our church communities might be able to live faithfully in them.

Reading is essential for the work of understanding our identity as churches that are seeking to embody Christ in our places. And our identity is interwoven with our vocation, and reading likewise is essential for discerning and maturing in our vocation, which we will explore in the next chapter.

four

Discerning Our Call

We have the vocation of infusing into the world,
whosoever we are, the sap and savor of Christianity.

DOROTHY DAY

My parents were both teachers: my mom an elementary school teacher, my dad a middle school math teacher. They taught me to read before I went to kindergarten. Even before I could read, they read to me and taught me to memorize Scripture and poetry. My journey of discerning a vocation began at home in those preschool years. Some of my earliest memories involve sitting on our secondhand couch as my mom read me the sometimes gruesome but compelling stories of Anabaptist martyrs from *The Martyrs Mirror*. These stories of radical Christian discipleship, alongside the scriptural stories that we read at home and at church, were the seeds of my Christian identity. They were the first faint whispers of the voice of Christ, calling me to follow him. And the stories my parents read to me were not limited to Scripture and tales of the martyrs. They also included classic children's novels, from the Chronicles of Narnia to *Charlotte's Web* to the Little House on the Prairie series and many others.

Throughout my childhood and adolescence, reading played an important part in the hopes and dreams I had for my life. As a young child, I wanted to be a firefighter in New York City. Although I can't remember any specific titles, this desire almost certainly stemmed from reading picture books about firefighters and about New York City. In elementary school, I learned quickly that I enjoyed and excelled at math and science. I loved our school's annual science fair and was an overachiever who spent months working on my project. I delighted in reading, experimenting and writing up my research. My love of science was also fueled in those early years by reading and rereading science fiction novels. I was particularly enthralled with the first two series of Tom Swift novels and with Eleanor Cameron's *Mushroom Planet* novels. In fifth grade I even started writing my own novel, inspired by Cameron's books.

I grew up in a conservative evangelical church. Although my theology today differs greatly from that of my childhood church, I was shaped by the supreme importance that my church placed on reading and understanding Scripture. Even in the early years of elementary school, I listened to and learned from our pastor's sermons. He was a master of slow, attentive reading. He spent years—what seemed like all of my childhood—preaching verse by verse through the books of 1 and 2 Corinthians.

When I was in fifth grade, our family moved into a house that was only a few blocks away from our town's public library. I was old enough then to walk to the library, and I spent a lot of my free time there, especially during the summers. The library's collection was relatively large for our town of well under ten thousand people. I reveled in the diversity of things to be read there: novels, magazines, newspapers, history, biographies, science, sports and more.

In middle school and high school, I continued to immerse myself in my science fair projects, becoming especially interested in prime numbers and their role in securing computer systems. Along the way, I read detailed papers in number theory and computer science and corresponded with leading scholars in these fields. I was growing certain that I was on a career track to do research in math or computer science.

Although I loved math and the burgeoning world of computers, I continued to enjoy reading broadly. I relished the novels that were assigned for my English classes. I was especially fascinated by the ways in which the diverse subjects that I was studying in school intersected with one another and with what I was reading and learning at church. In middle school I joined an adult class at our church that was studying theology on Sunday nights. There I encountered the basic ideas of ecclesiology, soteriology and pneumatology for the first time.

During my senior year of high school, I took an advanced placement course in nonfiction literature that would later play a crucial role in the shape of my vocation. It was in this class that I was introduced to the writings of Wendell Berry, Annie Dillard, Oliver Sacks, Barbara Tuchman and many other renowned essayists and nonfiction writers.

Following my dream of a career in math and computer science research, I chose to enroll in Taylor University, a tiny Christian liberal arts school with an extraordinary computer science department. I did well in all the courses of my major areas, but as my college years wore on, I found myself more inclined toward computer science than toward math. The courses I most enjoyed, however, were those in the honors program that explored the intersections of diverse areas of study: for instance, science and literature, faith and technology, the writings of C. S. Lewis and theology. My favorite course was one in the honors program,

titled Ways of Knowing, which I took during my very first se-
mester at Taylor. This wasn't an upper-level course in episte-
mology but a broad introduction to knowing that undoubtedly
left students with more questions than answers. We read mystery
novels (most notably ones by Dorothy Sayers) and were introduced to non-Euclidean geometries and logical syntax. We examined historical accounts and were challenged to consider the
roles of beauty and aesthetics in knowing.

After college I worked for a couple of years in information
technology. The familiar structure of the forty-hour work week
allowed me plenty of time to read. In these years I wrestled with
questions like what kind of church I should belong to and what
was the nature of the Christian faith to which I had committed
myself. One of the key books that I read and reread during this
phase of my life was Richard Foster's *Celebration of Discipline.*
This classic work not only articulates a call to a deeper life in
Christian community but also offers an abundant reading list in
the history of the Christian tradition. Inspired by Foster's work,
I devoured the writings of George Fox and other Quaker writers
but also the works of Thomas Merton, Dietrich Bonhoeffer,
Madame Guyon, St. John of the Cross and many others.

Growing weary of the rigidity of life in the corporate world,
I eventually decided to enroll in grad school. Pursuing a PhD
through a history and philosophy of science department offered me the wonderful opportunity to explore the intersections of a wide range of fields of study: history, philosophy,
mathematics, logic and many of the natural and social sciences. In the process I was exposed to the work of many
thinkers that I might not have otherwise read: from Aristotle
and Kant to Roger Bacon, Francis Bacon, Thomas Aquinas and
Isaac Newton, to Albert Einstein, Charles Darwin and David
Bohm. I didn't know it at the time, but I was getting the broad

education of a generalist that would serve me very well as the editor of a book review publication.

Reading has been essential for me in the work of discerning my vocation, as I have summarized here. It also has played a crucial role in the process of my beginning to mature in my vocation. I didn't set out be the editor of a book review magazine. Although I knew a little about blogs and online publishing, I knew next to nothing about publishing a print magazine. I have faced a steep learning curve as I struggle to grow and to do my work well. Reading has been perhaps the most important tool as I tackle this learning curve. I've read other book review publications and have learned from them. I've read blogs and other online publications and gotten ideas from them. I've read all sorts of how-to guides related to this work.

ORCHESTRATING OUR VOCATIONS IN THE LOCAL CHURCH

Questions of identity, as explored in the previous chapter, are integrally bound up with questions of vocation. Originating from the Latin verb *vocare*, meaning "to call," *vocation* is the term the church has used to describe our grappling with the call to follow Jesus and figuring out what sorts of work we are going to do along the way. Unfortunately, *vocation* today is often ripped from the context of the church community and is used almost exclusively to denote an individual's career path.

Vocation begins with Christ's call to follow him and with our choosing to follow that call. Our identity as followers of Christ, and as members of a local church community that seeks to embody Christ together, is the first and most significant element of our vocation. All other elements follow from our identity together in Christ. Although there is a meaningful sense in which each of us can speak of our personal vocation, as I have done above, we also should be attentive to the corporate vocation of our local church communities—that is, the work that we will engage in together and the ways in which our personal vocations complement and extend each other in this work. As an extension of our gratitude for the gifts God has provided in the people of our church community, our vocation together will take the shape of the gifts of our members.

If God is at work reconciling all things, then there is room for all kinds of gifts and skills within that mission. Certainly we need preachers and teachers and counselors, but our members and neighbors live in houses; the skills of architects and plumbers and carpenters can be leveraged in the work of the kingdom in caring for their housing needs. The skills of artists and poets and entrepreneurs and cooks and web designers all have their place as well. One of the primary roles of the local church, as Amy Sherman has argued in her book *Kingdom Calling*, is to discern and orchestrate all these skills in ways that bear witness to God's love and reconciliation.

What often is overlooked in our discernment of vocation is the vital role of the local church. When thinking about vocation, many Christians think of only two things: God's call to follow Jesus and their individual gifts and skills. If it is in the local church that we are to embody Christ together, as argued above, then it is within that context that we should discern how our individual skills can be made available for the shared work of bearing witness to the love and reconciliation of Christ.

One of the characteristics that distinguishes learning organizations from other sorts of social groups is that they have the ability to adapt to changing times while staying true to their primary mission. The leaders of Amazon.com, for instance, chose not to simply sell books, expanding first to a wide range of other goods, then to digital products like ebooks and music, and more recently to the production of electronic devices: ereaders, phones and television accessories. The present economic climate that churches face is precisely the sort of situation that beckons us to imagine new possibilities and to adapt. I recently participated in an online conversation in which pastors from around North America were lamenting that churches are increasingly unable to afford full-time pastoral positions. Many prospective pastors are saddled with heavy debt loads from their undergraduate and seminary studies and need full-time employment to keep up with their bills. Faced with this sort of economic quandary, our churches need to think outside the economic traditions we have inherited. If we are willing to work together in ways that generate income, most churches will have the resources to either hire a full-time pastor or create meaningful part-time work that could supplement a pastor's income. As our churches seek to be learning organizations that can adapt to changing situations, reading books like Luther Snow's helpful work *The Power of Asset-Mapping* can stir our imaginations about the ways in which we understand and implement vocation within the local church economy.

As a small urban congregation with a massive building to maintain, my own local church was thrust early into the sort of economic uncertainty that many churches are facing today. We have been wrestling with these challenges for almost twenty years. Through practices of reading and conversation, we have been fortunate enough to have cultivated a little imagination regarding the shared economy of our church. We have started several businesses that use the gifts of our members to benefit our neighborhood and other churches. These include a daycare and preschool, a community development corporation engaged in affordable housing and economic development, and the *Englewood Review of Books*, which recommends resources for our church and other churches around the world. These businesses provide common work for us, employing people in full- and part-time positions and involving many others as volunteers. This common work allows a growing number of our members to be together on a daily basis, working with each other and thinking and talking often about how our faith gets lived out amidst all the wonderful assets and deep challenges of our neighborhood. Not all churches are in a position to start businesses. Even here at Englewood, a relatively small percentage of the adults in our congregation are employed by our businesses. But there are at least a dozen nonprofit and for-profit organizations in our neighborhood that we partner with and that employ (or have employed) our members. We have a doctor who works at the local health clinic, a bookkeeper who works for another community development organization, several folks who work for the neighborhood food co-op, several others who work for a homeless ministry in our neighborhood, and many others. Having members who work for these groups has opened the doors to facilitate better and deeper partnerships between them and our church.

Other people in our congregation who don't work in our businesses or partner organizations make their skills available for the work of the church. A landscaper does work—sometimes for pay and sometimes not—on our church property and other properties that the church owns. A wonderful group of retired men and women show up at the church building on most days of the week to do whatever work needs to be done on that day, from taking out the trash to painting to driving people on errands.

Common work, members who work for partner organizations and members who offer their skills for the work of the church—these are all facets of the vocation that are discerning in our particular church community. Other churches will find different ways of orchestrating the gifts and skills of their members. If our churches are to mature in our embodiment of Jesus, then we need to be aware of members' talents and skills and continually be finding creative ways to orchestrate these gifts not only to sustain our congregation in tumultuous economic times but also to bear witness to the good news of Jesus.

DISCERNING VOCATION

As I emphasized in telling my story at the beginning of this chapter, reading is essential to the nurturing of vocation in two particular ways: in the discernment of vocation and especially in the work of maturing within a vocation. If discerning our identity, as discussed in the previous chapter, is about the question "Who are we?" then discerning vocation is about the question "What are we going to do?" There are two levels at which this question must be answered—that of the church as a whole and that of individual members—and reading plays a crucial role on both of them.

Reading can serve as a guide as we discern our congregational vocation, seeking to answer the related questions "How are we going to be involved in the life of our neighborhood?" and "Specifically, what kind of work are we going to do here?" As some churches consider the possibility of common work, they might read stories of Christian communities that have done common work, their rationale for doing so and the challenges that they met along the way. The monastic tradition, and particularly the Benedictine order, has a rich history of working together, and books like *Holy Work* by Dom Rembert Sorg can be really helpful for churches in imagining the possibilities of common work. If we discern that our church has been called to common work, we will have to learn the legal and financial ropes of a church doing business. Hopefully we will have friends (inside the congregation or outside it) who can guide us, but readings about these aspects of common work can also serve as a guide. As we survey the organizations that we might consider partnering with, we will inevitably read to learn more about them, both the particular organization, as we seek to understand its history and mission, and also the broader sorts of work that these groups do: feeding and sheltering the homeless, tutoring children or running a farmer's market, for instance.

In his essential book on vocation *Let Your Life Speak*, Parker Palmer notes that discerning a personal vocation "does not come from willfulness. It comes from listening."[1] The art of listening that we cultivate in our life together through practices of slow and careful reading (recall chapter one) will serve us well as we seek to discern our vocations as churches and individuals. As a church, we listen to our neighbors and to our place, seeking to discern where God is already at work and how we can begin to follow God's leading in our neighborhood. We also listen to our members, tuning our ears and our eyes for the sorts of work in which they find joy and become most alive.

In discerning our personal vocations, we should—as Palmer suggests—listen to our lives, being attentive to the desires that God has given us and the ways in which we pursue these desires. Is our pursuit leading us deeper into koinonia, the abundant shared life that God intends for creation? Books like Jen Pollock Michel's *Teach Us to Want* and James K. A. Smith's *Desiring the Kingdom* can be particularly helpful in our efforts to understand our desires and how—if we will listen carefully—they will gently guide us deeper into the way of Jesus. The poet John O'Donohue has noted the connection between beauty and calling, and indeed it is often through beauty that God calls to us. As we read well-crafted creative works—fiction, nonfiction and especially poetry—our eyes and ears are trained to recognize the beauty that surrounds us and to discern God's voice within the beautiful.

In discerning our personal vocation, we should also listen to our church community. What work is already under way in our life together that we can joyfully immerse ourselves in? We also should listen to brothers and sisters in our church, as sometimes they will be able to hear the call of our life better than we can. In the Quaker tradition, the clearness committee is a practice of gathering sisters and brothers for discernment that creates an intentional space in which others can listen to our life with us and ask questions that help clarify our calling at a particular time. Writings on clearness committees from Quaker authors like Richard Foster and Parker Palmer can help us imagine what practices of intentional listening to one another might look like within our particular congregation.

In discerning a personal vocation, we also should listen closely to the economy of our life. What are the measures by which we determine our standard of living? All too often we simply default to setting our standard of living as high as possible, choosing a career that will maximize our income and then living within (or sometimes even beyond) those means. As we seek to discern our own standard of living, we should listen (and pay attention) to our neighbors. Is our standard of living similar to that of our neighbors? Instead of living at the highest possible standard, perhaps we might consider a standard of living that will allow us to maximize our generosity— the amount of time and money we devote to the care of others and to the flourishing of our church and neighborhood. Books like Richard Rohr's *Simplicity: The Freedom of Letting Go* and Richard Foster's *The Freedom of Simplicity* can help us think about our personal and family economy in ways that offer an alternative to the crass consumerism that dominates Western culture.

Reading will also inevitably play a role in the work of helping individuals discern a personal vocation within the church community. Thomas Merton has written that a person "knows when he has found his vocation when he stops thinking about how to live and begins to live. . . . When we find our vocation—thought and life are one."[2] From preschool on, we expose our children to stories that portray all sorts of work. We read Scripture with them, introducing them to the story of God's reconciling mission in creation, and gently invite them to hear and follow the call of Christ. We watch patiently over time to see the kinds of work that our children are drawn toward. We also should help our young people understand their unique personalities and strengths (with tests like the Enneagram and Myers-Briggs) and the significance of the personality of each as it pertains to work. We pay attention to the books they read (and the music they listen to and the movies and television shows they watch), talking with them about the stories that they find compelling. We also listen to the desires that are taking shape in their hearts. All of this involves reading and conversation.

As a young person is drawn into a particular kind of work, we can offer resources to read that take a deeper look at that type of work and how it relates to our faith. Such resources could include both nonfiction and fiction.

- One feeling drawn toward nursing, for instance, might be encouraged to read a biography or two of Florence Nightingale; one drawn toward the visual arts might be encouraged to read Chaim Potok's novel *The Gift of Asher Lev*.

- Youth who are interested in writing or teaching literature might read Karen Swallow Prior's *Fierce Convictions: The Extraordinary Life of Hannah More*.

- Those interested in the sciences might read some of John Polkinghorne's writings on Christian faith and science.

- Students interested in the culinary arts might be encouraged to read Michael Schut's *Food and Faith* or Shauna Niequist's *Bread and Wine*.

MATURING IN A VOCATION

In a similar fashion, reading can not only help us discern vocation but also help us mature in our particular vocation. Regardless of the work that we have been called to do—whether one is a plumber, a teacher, an auto mechanic, an engineer or a lawyer—reading will help us to better understand our work and assist us in doing it more skillfully. If we desire to do our work well, we will learn from others who are doing similar work by reading trade publications, including technical manuals, how-to guides and journals. We also are called to a deeper knowledge of how our work is integrated in our local congregation with the mission of God and the work of our sisters and brothers.

Listening is an important part not just of discerning vocation but also of maturing into a vocation. We listen and watch for opportunities to use our gifts and skills in ways that are more integrated with the life of our church and neighborhood. Sometimes opportunities will arise within the ongoing shared work of the church. Other times we will need to imagine new sorts of opportunities into which we could enter. Reading the stories and reflections of others who have similar gifts and skills can be vital to imagining new opportunities.

- Those in the medical professions, for example, might read *The Body of Compassion* or other books by Joel Shuman.

- Architects and those in construction and real estate trades might read Philip Bess's *Till We Have Built Jerusalem* or Eric Jacobsen's *The Space Between*, both of which offer a theology of the built environment.

- Visual artists should read books like *God in the Gallery* by Daniel Siedell.

- Those in pastoral vocations might read and reflect on Eugene Peterson's memoir *The Pastor*.

- Teachers should read and reflect on the works of Parker Palmer, especially his book *The Courage to Teach.*

Mentoring relationships can be helpful ways of listening as we seek to mature in a vocation. Being mentored by someone in our congregation—or in another local congregation—who has a similar vocation and who is willing to share their wisdom is particularly helpful for the work of maturing into our own personal vocations. The people who work for Englewood Community Development Corporation, which is based in my local church, have benefited greatly from the wisdom of Reba Place Fellowship, which has been doing community development work for much longer than we have in an urban neighborhood that is fairly similar to ours. We should also be willing to mentor younger brothers and sisters who are in earlier phases of maturing into their vocation. Books like *Deep Mentoring* by Randy Reese and Robert Loane are wonderful resources for helping us understand the role of mentoring as we mature in a vocation.

Sometimes discerning our vocation and maturing into a vocation go hand in hand. "Our vocation is not a sphinx's riddle," observes Merton in his classic book *No Man Is an Island*, "which we must solve in one guess or else perish."[3] Merton goes on to note that some people have the paradoxical vocation of constantly seeking their vocation. We should take care not to identify too strongly with our vocation, and must grant others the same grace, so that as we mature as churches and individuals we may continue to follow Christ through changing desires, changing landscapes and changing economies.

Reading undoubtedly leads us deeper into our identity and vocation as church communities. With the scriptural story as our primary guide, and many other resources that help us clarify and embody that story, we are led by the Holy Spirit toward deeper faithfulness. The fruits of this faithfulness will be tiny tastes of the flourishing that God intends for all humanity and all creation. Reading is thus essential not only to the flourishing of our church communities but to the flourishing of our neighborhoods, as we will explore in the next two chapters.

five
·····

Reading with Our Neighbors

*In prayer and contemplation we begin to understand that our
identity is not to be found in our differences from others—in our
superiorities and inferiorities—but in our common humanity.*

PARKER J. PALMER

I n his acclaimed book *How the Irish Saved Civilization,* Thomas
Cahill brings to life a little-known chapter in history, the half-
millennium from the fall of the Roman Empire in the fifth
century to the rise of medieval Europe. The characters at the
heart of the story are the Irish monastics, whose work of preserving and disseminating Latin texts was vital to the perpetu-
ation of Western civilization.

Cahill begins with St. Patrick. It was Patrick who converted
Ireland to Christianity, and this conversion was unique for its
time as "the first de-Romanized Christianity in human history,
a Christianity without the sociopolitical baggage of the Greco-
Roman world, a Christianity that completely inculturated itself
into the Irish scene."[1] Although Irish Christianity after Patrick

was "de-Romanized," Cahill emphasizes that there was one element of Roman Christianity that the Irish retained: literacy.
Irish monasticism arose not long after Ireland's conversion to
Christianity. Monks eventually founded universities that, in the
spirit of Irish hospitality, welcomed anyone who wanted to learn,
regardless of economic status or whether that person was called
to a monastic vocation. Not only were students taught how to
read in the university, but a wide range of texts were copied out
painstakingly by hand, from theological works to those of pagan
Greco-Roman culture to the traditional stories of Ireland. Cahill
says that although the monks would get grumpy at times, they
generally found a deep joy in copying texts: "[They] engaged the
text they were working on, tried to comprehend it after their
fashion, and, if possible, add to it, even improve on it. In this
dazzling new culture, a book was not an isolated document on
a dusty shelf; book truly spoke to book, and writer to scribe, and
scribe to reader, from one generation to the next."[2]

At the same time that the tools and habits of literacy were
rising in Ireland in the sixth century, literacy on the European
continent was in rapid decline. Libraries were being destroyed,
and the role of the scribe waned and vanished, ensuring that the
libraries would not be replaced. Over the next few centuries,
however, Irish monks would push deeper and deeper into con-
tinental Europe, planting monasteries and universities along the
way. Through this Irish missionary movement that spread texts
and the love of learning across the then-desolate continent of
Europe, Western civilization was saved.

Cahill's story reminds us that reading is essential for healthy,
flourishing cultures. It also helps us see that our churches stand
within a long history of Christian communities that have functioned as learning communities in which practices of reading
and learning were interwoven with habits of caring for members

of the community and neighbors. If we take this history seriously, church communities in the twenty-first century could be well positioned to cultivate habits of literacy that foster life in their particular places.

CHURCHES AND THE FLOURISHING OF OUR PLACES

Before we delve into the role of literacy in caring for the health and well-being of our places, it would be beneficial to remind ourselves that the seeking of God's *shalom* (that is, peace and flourishing) in our neighborhoods is essential to our identity as churches following in the way of Jesus. In the twenty-first century, when not only churches but also many neighborhoods are formed by a profound placelessness, it is easy for us to lose sight of our call to love our neighbors in tangible and sustainable ways and to work alongside them, seeking the flourishing of our place together.

One refrain that echoes throughout the New Testament is the instruction to "live peaceably" with our neighbors, even those we might consider enemies (for example, Matthew 5:43-48; Romans 12:17-21; Colossians 3:12-17; Hebrews 12:14-29). When we read these passages, we must bear in mind that the majority of first-century Christians were Jews by birth, with a concept of peace that was much broader than the mere "absence of conflict" that comes to mind when we as twenty-first-century Westerners hear the word. Taking the New Testament as a whole, we get a robust sense of what it means to love and be at peace with our neighbors. Perhaps one of the richest explanations of seeking the peace of our places can be found in Romans 12:17-21 (note the italicized phrases):

> *Do not repay anyone evil for evil,* but take thought for what is noble in the sight of all. If it is possible, so far as it depends on you, *live peaceably with all.* Beloved, *never avenge yourselves,* but leave room for the wrath of God; for it is

written, "Vengeance is mine, I will repay, says the Lord." No, *"if your enemies are hungry, feed them*; if they are thirsty, give them something to drink; for by doing this you will heap burning coals on their heads." *Do not be overcome by evil, but overcome evil with good.*

The first-century Roman church would have been largely composed of ethnic Jews, living in a city dominated at the time by a pagan Gentile culture that was largely hostile toward both Jews and Christians. This passage from Paul's letter speaks directly to the heart of the Roman church's situation; its daily life unfolded among enemies. Even in that situation, Paul calls the members of the church to live generously—sharing their food and drink, for instance. The peace of Christ that they were called to embody not only was generous but, in overcoming evil with good, transformed hostility into goodwill. Our places are transformed as we embody a peace that gently wins over our neighbors and draws them into peaceful ways of living and sharing.

Dwight Friesen, Tim Soerens and Paul Sparks, in their groundbreaking book *The New Parish*, articulate what churches are called to embody in their particular places as "faithful presence." The theological groundwork for faithful presence, they contend, lies in an understanding of what it means to live *within* our place. They explain:

> By within we mean standing in solidarity with your neighbors who have a shared desire to see your place be a good place to live. Within is about rooting in your context. You and all your neighbors desire clean air to breathe, good schools for your children, livable vocations that serve the common good, justice for all, a voice in how things are governed, and so on. You and all your neighbors want to learn and be wise, have the opportunity to grow and be healthy: physically, emotionally,

spiritually, relationally. The gospel bids us to seek the flourishing of life for all.[3]

Our call as churches to seek "the flourishing of life for all" is the theological conviction that will guide us in this chapter. Two pertinent questions arise as we seek to understand the role of reading and literacy in seeking the flourishing of our places: (1) How does literacy contribute to the flourishing of our places? and (2) how are churches well suited to participate in cultivating literacy to promote flourishing?

Although literacy contributes to the flourishing of our places in many ways, let's focus for now on two specific ways that emerge in Cahill's history of the Irish monks. First, literacy helps *preserve* the memory of a place, which we might call the *library function*. Although preliterate oral cultures do have a kind of memory, there is necessarily a limit and an elasticity to this memory; each generation tells the culture's inherited stories in its own way. In contrast, libraries have a more extensive and more specific memory. Think, for example, of the Irish monks who, while copying texts and building libraries, preserved the memories of the Greek and Roman Empires. Having a memory of the past is vital to the work of forging a strong identity, which in turn is necessary for the flourishing of our places. "Those who cannot remember the past," George Santayana famously said, "are condemned to repeat it."[4]

The second essential way that literacy contributes to flourishing can be called the *education function*. If the goal of the library function is to preserve, the goal of the education function is to *equip* people to read and to contribute in meaningful ways to the flourishing of their places. As the Irish monks' missionary work carried them deeper into Europe, they taught the pagan peoples of that continent how to read and write. Teaching people how to read and write—literacy, in the barest sense—is a good start. But cultural literacy—teaching people how to participate in cultivating the common good—can't be neglected either.

Beyond the habits of literacy, Cahill does not probe too deeply into the monastic life of the Irish missionaries, but I think it is significant that these scribes were monks whose way of life was rooted in a community of people being formed to seek an all-encompassing common good. In their monastic life they were modeling a sort of learning organization in which reading and learning were intertwined with neighborly care. The monks' habits of study, and especially their reading of Scripture and theological works, shaped the ways in which they engaged their neighbors and enabled their places to flourish.

LIBRARIES

Churches can make important contributions to the health and flourishing of their places in the arenas of both libraries and education. Many churches already have congregational libraries, which benefit their members. However, in order to benefit the well-being of their places, churches should think more broadly about libraries. I would like to suggest two significant ways in which a church could play a vital role in cultivating libraries.

First, if they already have a congregational library, they might consider broadening its focus, making it a resource for the residents of their neighborhood. This approach would be particularly compelling in rural areas or other places without existing public libraries. Broadening the focus of the church library does not mean that you should spend large amounts of money acquiring the latest pop novels and self-help books that a public library might offer. Rather, the first focus should be on broadening your library's *audience*. Publicize the fact that the library is available to the public. Find ways to get neighbors outside the church to make use of the library. Inevitably the scope of the library's collection will broaden at least a little over time, but the church should be stay focused on resources that help promote the common good of the place. Some of the areas in which the library might broaden its collection beyond a typical congregational library include books on community building, how-to books on skills and crafts that contribute to the flourishing of a place (gardening, landscaping, auto mechanics, arts, etc.), books on local history and culture, and works of fiction and poetry that are written by local authors or that inspire the reader to reflect on his or her situation and to become more deeply engaged in the life of the place.

One church that has opened its library to the public is First Church of Christ Congregational in West Hartford, Connecticut. Its John P. Webster Library contains a "diverse collection of religious and secular resources and services to engage religious and spiritual growth, inspiration, learning and fellowship for all ages."[5] The library, funded through the generosity of a philanthropist in the congregation, has two staff people. It offers neighbors not only books but also programming that includes book discussion groups and an art gallery.

A second way in which a church might help promote local libraries is to support the work of an existing public library (or the library of a nearby university or seminary whose collections are open to the public). Churches can promote local libraries in a variety of ways. Above all, churches that want to support a library should encourage members and neighbors to use the library. Many libraries leverage usage statistics to make a case for additional funding or at least to better allocate their funding. Additionally, many libraries have Friends of the Library groups. A church could appoint liaisons to this group, who would keep the church aware of what's going on at the library and how the church can be involved. Libraries are often eager to have volunteers who help with programming or other necessary work that supplements the efforts of library staff. Churches also should be advocates for libraries when they face threats of closure or funding cuts.

Here at Englewood Christian Church, we are fortunate to have a branch of the Indianapolis Public Library less than a block from our building. We have been involved on many levels with this library. For example, we have volunteered there and rallied neighbors to fight for this branch when it was threatened with closure. We also take classes from our preschool there for educational programs. We have recently partnered with the library and other neighbors to develop plans to allow it to expand its facilities and make them more accessible. This expansion would make it better prepared to sustain its services in the coming decades.

CHURCHES AND THE WORK OF EDUCATION

Besides supporting libraries, churches can also support literacy education, as the ancient Irish monastics did. In fact, Sunday school began in England in the 1780s—before the age of public education—as a way for churches to teach children to read on their day off work. Today we might have a school or preschool that teaches children to read. Or we might have Sunday school classes or other groups that teach children and adults to read Scripture (and other works) in communion, as described in chapter three. Organizing community book groups, for instance, can be an effective way for us to engage our neighbors in practices of reading in communion: reading together and allowing the reading to guide us into conversations about the shared life of our neighborhood.

Churches should also be eager to support literacy among their neighbors. This support might include volunteering at a school or with a literacy group that teaches adults to read. Here in Indianapolis, a nonprofit group called City Mosaic helps churches partner with struggling Indianapolis public schools by providing volunteers who tutor students in reading and other skills essential for learning. Teaching our neighbors to read is an essential first step on their journey toward being well prepared to contribute to the flourishing of our place.

Neil Gaiman emphasizes that literacy—and especially reading fiction—is essential because it builds our capacity for empathy. "You get to feel things, visit places and worlds you would never otherwise know. [In reading fiction] you're being someone else, and when you return to your own world, you're going to be slightly changed. Empathy is a tool for building people into groups, for allowing us to function as more than self-obsessed individuals."[6] Neighbors who cannot read can participate in and contribute to working toward the flourishing of our place, but there will be severe limits to their participation. As Gaiman observes, reading helps us all to overcome those limits and to be empathetic in the ways we interact.

Frank Laubach was a well-known twentieth-century missionary who worked among the Maranao people of the Philippines in the 1930s. Here he came to learn that literacy was an essential component of development, a first step toward working together toward the flourishing of their place—and he thus became convinced that literacy education goes hand in hand with the mission of the church. Laubach developed a literacy method he called "each one teach one." As people "learned to read, they would, in turn, teach other adults on a one-to-one basis."[7]

Laubach saw literacy as essential to establishing the *shalom* of God. One 1968 newspaper article declared: "Frank Laubach, world citizen and prophet of literacy, has a practical solution to the problem of world peace; he proposes to mobilize the world church as a vast army against illiteracy and poverty."[8] In 1954 Laubach wrote,

The hungry people of the world want *more than charity*, they want to *be helped to help themselves*. They want to be able to raise bigger crops on their land; they want land of their own; they want credit banks so that they can borrow money without paying terrible rates of interest. They want to get rid of disease. Help them help themselves. This is what the Church ought to be doing *on a very large scale*.[9]

Literacy, Laubach believed, was the crucial first step in this process of helping people to help themselves.

Although we need to be careful not to equate the kingdom of God with American capitalist democracy—a charge some critics raised about Laubach's work[10]—developing literate and educated citizens that are prepared to engage in the work of helping their places flourish is a reasonable end toward which our churches should be moving in our engagement with our neighbors. In pursuing this end, we also should be guided by a deep sense of our own immaturity in being educated for and engaged in the life of our particular place.

Civic Literacy and Civic Engagement

The founding fathers of the United States understood education as essential to the preservation of democracy. Thomas Jefferson was particularly emphatic about it. He wrote in a letter to James Madison: "Educate and inform the whole mass of the people, enable them to see that it is their interest to preserve peace and order, and they will preserve it. . . . They are the only sure reliance for the preservation of our liberty."[11]

Literacy is the basis for all other forms of education. We read to learn more about history, science, theology, government. Almost any facet of learning in the modern era involves reading. Knowledge, however, is insufficient if it does not lead us into civic engagement, into the work of caring for our places. US Representative Lee Hamilton has said:

> Citizenship requires both knowledge about government and the ability to be involved in governance. It means knowing how to identify and inform yourself about issues, explore and evaluate possible solutions, and then act to resolve problems. It demands that you know how to interact respectfully with others. And it asks that you accept responsibility for meeting your community's and the nation's challenges.[12]

The best way for churches to help promote civic literacy and engagement is to practice it—and not only to practice it but to invite our neighbors into public conversations about issues. Invite not only your members but also your neighbors to take part in these conversations. Churches are well suited to tackle some of the challenges that might prohibit some neighbors from participating in public conversations. For instance, if neighbors are unable to participate because they have small children who can't be left at home, we can provide childcare during public meetings. If some of our neighbors do not speak English, we can help find interpreters.

If neighbors are still unable or unwilling to attend public conversations, we can engage the issues with them on a personal basis, over coffee or a meal, or simply in front-porch conversations. Civic conversation has become such a foreign practice in North America (as documented in monumental books such as Robert Putnam's *Bowling Alone* or Bill Bishop's *The Big Sort*) that some neighbors may not know how to enter into it. In my church's experience of conversing and working toward the flourishing of our place, we have found that it is easier to get our neighbors involved in this work, and to keep them involved, when the focus is positive and not negative. Instead of always

entering public conversations with an oppositional stance—
energized by the things we are *against*—we do well to work for
a positive vision *for* the future of our place, pursuing the collective hopes and dreams of our neighbors.

Chapter two introduced the concept of the social imagination.
The neighborhood—however large or small—is where the social
imagination comes to life. The odds of a single church or group
of neighbors changing the world are pretty slim. With some de-
termination, however, neighbors can make local changes that
help their place inch forward toward health and flourishing. In
the next chapter we will consider some of the ways in which we
can move toward a deeper shared life in our neighborhoods and
the place reading has in the process.

six

Deepening Our Roots in
Our Neighborhoods

*A community cannot be made or preserved apart from
the loyalty and affection of its members and the
respect and goodwill of the people outside it.*

WENDELL BERRY

Tim Soerens, one of the coauthors of *The New Parish*, tells a
story of living in Seattle's South Lake Union neighborhood
at a time when it was undergoing massive redevelopment
funded by one of Microsoft's cofounders. As he began to participate in meetings related to this redevelopment, Soerens was
struck by how everyone involved in the process seemed to be
driven by their own interests and not that of the neighborhood
as a whole. He writes:

> Whether there were four people in the room or forty, it
> quickly became obvious to everyone precisely why they
> were they were there. One person was representing low-

income housing, another trying to build a dog park, another was chiefly concerned about the building heights and so on. What also became obvious is that no one in the room seemed to care about the neighborhood as a whole. Everyone was so focused on the outcome they were representing that a competition sometimes emerged. The question [I found myself] asking was, "How are they going to fit together as a team for the mutual flourishing of the neighborhood?"[1]

Through his advocacy for the neighborhood as a whole, Tim built trust with those who were working on the neighborhood redevelopment. As a result, millions of dollars were invested in low-income housing in that rapidly gentrifying neighborhood, which preserved the possibility that it could be a diverse, flourishing place.

As our church has worked in community development in a very different sort of neighborhood on the Near Eastside of Indianapolis, we have had similar experiences. We regularly encounter groups and individuals that are largely driven by the desire to make things work out as well as possible for themselves, with little thought for the neighborhood as a whole. Sometimes we have mediated difficult situations with disagreeing groups that refused to collaborate. We urge these conflicting parties to see that cooperation would be in the best interest of everyone.

For communities whose life is shaped by the story of God reconciling *all* things in creation, experiences like these remind us that churches can be well situated to catalyze the flourishing of a particular place as a whole. But what does it look like for us to move deeper into the sort of holistic flourishing that God intends for our neighborhoods? This movement begins in our imaginations, with the dreams we have of what the flourishing of our place will look like. Even in an age when many places are losing their distinctiveness and people pack up and move in a heartbeat, everyone has dreams about the neighborhood in which they want to live. Granted, for many people a healthy neighborhood means little more than rising property values. Although such a vision is fueled by self-interest, it is still a dream for the flourishing of the place.

Maybe we'd like to see better bike routes or more cooperation between local artists or local farmers. Perhaps we'd like to see that empty lot on the corner turned into a park or a garden. Maybe our dream is to be able to walk to work or to the grocery store, or to have a thriving arts scene. All of these are dreams for flourishing. Most likely business and government leaders in your neighborhood already have a plan for progressing and developing toward some form of flourishing. Have you seen and read that plan? Do you know who stewards it and how you can participate in helping the plan to change and mature?

READING AND OUR DREAMS FOR OUR NEIGHBORHOODS

For individuals or for neighborhoods, the journey from dream to reality is often a circuitous one. We will encounter mountains that we have to circumvent or rivers that will drive us many miles out of our way to cross. How do our dreams become realities?

Work is the primary means by which we realize our dreams. In seeking the flourishing of our neighborhood, very specialized kinds of work will often be required: the skills of the architect, the lawyer, the real estate broker, for instance. Reading is an essential skill for this journey. It helps us understand the kinds of work that will need to go into realizing a particular dream in our neighborhood. Reading will also help us to understand and converse with those who will do the most skilled and intensive parts of the work.

Sometimes reading can directly help us fulfill a dream for our neighborhood. For instance, if we wanted to transform a vacant lot into a garden or a bird sanctuary, there are books that can help us make this dream a reality. If we think our neighborhood needs more knitters, there are books that can help us with the logistics of starting a knitting class.

Other times pursuing a shared dream for our neighborhood is not so simple. If we are going to build any kind of structure— say a playground, a shed or a house—we will likely need a building permit. We will have to read building and planning codes to find out what kind of permissions are necessary. Then, of course, once the permits are obtained we can read how to build the structure well, if we intend to build it ourselves.

Larger projects will likely involve the work of professionals— architects, engineers, ecologists, planners, contractors, grant writers. Even though others may be doing the highly specialized work, it's helpful to know how to talk to them as we coordinate the project. Each area of specialization inevitably has its own jargon. We learn to navigate this jargon by reading online or print resources, which helps us communicate most effectively with those who are doing the work. Not everyone needs to be familiar with all types of jargon, of course. But we do need people in our church or neighborhood who can communicate with professionals and help coordinate the work that needs to be done.

We might also read stories of people in other places who had similar dreams and how their dreams were realized. One of my favorite picture books is Peter Brown's *The Curious Garden*. Inspired by the story of the High Line Park in New York City, Brown tells the compelling story of young Liam, who dreams of bringing color to the dreary city in which he lives. Liam, who is quite the young explorer, stumbles upon an unused railway bed on which some colorful wildflowers have popped up. He begins to tend these flowers, and the railway garden grows. Other gardeners soon join the effort. Before long the gardens spill over and saturate the whole city, realizing Liam's dream of a vibrant, colorful city that is full of life. Stories like this not only spark our imaginations but guide us into the work of realizing the shared dreams that we have for our neighborhood.

READING TO UNDERSTAND OUR PLACE

In order to begin realizing the shared dreams that we have for our neighborhood, we need a robust understanding of our place. This sort of knowledge will help us assess the feasibility of our dreams and also will assist in prioritizing our pursuit of them. Some dreams may need to be fulfilled before others can be explored. Some dreams may not be feasible in the short run because we do not have the necessary resources.

Neighbors here in the Englewood neighborhood of Indianapolis, for instance, have a shared dream of a walkable neighborhood. This future we imagine, however, is a long-term objective. In order to move in this direction, we have many more immediate objectives that need to be realized. These near-term goals include increasing population density, increasing job opportunities, increasing walkable retail outlets, adapting roads and infrastructure to accommodate the shift from automobility to walkability. The key to a neighborhood's being able to assess and organize its dreams is the depth of residents' understanding of the place they inhabit.

Chapter three discussed the role of reading in shaping our identity as churches: exploring who and why and how and when we are. There is another facet of our identity—the question of *where* we are—that I intentionally saved for this chapter, because it is a question best pursued alongside our neighbors, not apart from them. Churches can be a profound asset to their neighborhoods by working with neighbors to cultivate a deep working understanding of their particular place.

The identity of our place is always in flux, changing as we work with our neighbors toward flourishing. I had the opportunity several years ago to interview the prominent theologian Willie James Jennings, who teaches black church history and theology (among other things) at Duke Divinity School. I asked him how urban churches like mine in Indianapolis can foster deeper connections with the land, with our neighbors and with our place. He responded:

> Part of what's necessary in urban areas is to recognize that these areas are caught up in this horrific cycle of ever-overturning of space, so that it has no real sense of continuity. So the question becomes, what does it mean to try to create a form of continuity where lives actually matter in the midst of space that by its very nature and definition resists that kind of continuity? My hope for churches is that they might be communities of faith that claim habitation of such space, learn its history, become in many ways if it is possible . . . a church that could tell the history of the place; a church that honors the history of the place, and not simply honoring the history of the place, but honoring the people that have been there. I hope that [these sort of practices] would set the stage for imaging ways to honor the people who are currently there, who may not be a part of that history but might be invited to see themselves as a part of that history, who are not necessarily of the same identity of those who are currently sharing in the legacy of that location. . . . [Often in urban areas a] sense of continuity, a legacy is not there. After people die, property is taken, changed and transformed, and it moves on in a new

incarnation. Unfortunately, what you have in many cases is
that the precious memories of people's lives are not carried
on by anyone, and who better than the church to find a way
to claim hold of those legacies? And I would hope that any
attempt to think about urban space would include that.[2]

Although Jennings and I were discussing urban places, churches
can play a similar role in rural or suburban places. The practices
that Jennings advocates here are reminiscent of the Irish monastics and could be described in terms of the library and education functions introduced in the previous chapter. In cultivating
libraries, a church should collect resources that preserve the
memory of the place with integrity. In working to educate ourselves and our neighbors, we teach the story of our place, as well
as habits that will help to preserve its legacy.

Reading is an essential practice in the work of uncovering
and preserving the legacy of our places. There are many facets
to this reading that may appeal to different people in our church
communities. History is one important facet. Reading local
history can help us understand why our place has taken the
shape that it has. Through reading we can uncover the role that
regional, state and national history have played in giving form
to our place. Oral histories from older neighbors who have lived
in this place for a long time have a special value. In fact, a church
can cultivate the memory of its neighborhood by collecting and
preserving books, photographs and other documents that help
to tell its story.

Churches also can play an educational role in the work of local
history: hosting storytelling events about the neighborhood or
teaching neighbors how to record oral history or to carry out
other practices that help to preserve the legacy of a place.
Churches might even publish their own works on local history

on a blog or perhaps even in print. Several years ago, for instance, I coordinated a project to write a short book on the history of our Englewood neighborhood. This history book combined oral and written histories with a rich collection of historical documents and photographs. Every homeowner in our neighborhood was given a copy of this volume, and today the book continues to provide opportunities for us to leverage our past as we work toward the flourishing of our neighborhood.

Another facet of cultivating the legacy of our place is understanding local economics. Economics of course is closely tied to history: what are the businesses or industries that have sustained and given shape to this place? But even beyond historical studies, reading can help us understand how these industries functioned—where the employees and raw materials came from and how certain industries interacted with one another.

Ecology is another vital facet of knowing our place. Reading books in conjunction with "reading" the environment can help us understand the land, climate, water systems, flora and fauna of our place. "The best nature writing, as I conceive of it," wrote twentieth-century poet and naturalist Liberty Hyde Bailey, "is that which portrays the commonplace so truthfully and so clearly that the reader forthwith goes out to see for himself."[3] Bailey goes on to say that the conjoined practices of reading and natural observation are essential tools for one seeking to know his place: "[This approach] gives him point of view; tells him what to look for; enables him to look beneath the surface; trains his judgment as to causes and effects; guides him in distinguishing the essential; saves him from humiliating error."[4]

Our focus in understanding the ecology of our place, Bailey notes, should be on the weather and the landscape, which consists for him of "three elements—the surface of the earth, the sky, the vegetation."[5] As we come to understand the climate and the landscape of our place, we grow in our knowledge of the context within which we must flourish.

As we read to understand our place, our reading does not have to be restricted to nonfiction. Novels often help us understand facets of our places in more compelling and memorable ways than nonfiction. Wendell Berry's novels, for instance, offer keen insight into the culture of rural Kentucky, and rural places in general. *Great Expectations* and other novels by Charles Dickens help us understand London in the nineteenth century. Similarly, Flannery O'Connor's stories illuminate life in Georgia—and perhaps other parts of the Deep South—in the mid-twentieth century.

Poetry and drama also can help us understand our place, particularly the local language that identifies it. Maurice Manning's poetry, for instance, vividly portrays the dialect of contemporary Kentucky. Here in central Indiana, the works of early twentieth-century poet James Whitcomb Riley convey the distinct dialect of our region in that era. In fact, his poetry is almost unreadable today because so much of the dialect has been lost. However, his poems illuminate some current Indiana colloquialisms that are vestiges of this earlier dialect.

Our churches can collect literary works and preserve the literary legacy of our place. And if we have skilled writers in our congregation or neighborhood, we should encourage them to teach other neighbors to write fiction and poetry that is deeply rooted in our place.

Cultivating the Commons

As we grow in understanding our place, we can begin the work of helping it to flourish in informed and meaningful ways. One essential part of working toward the flourishing of our place is cultivating the commons. The commons has been defined simply as "all that we share," and in the twenty-first century, when so much of our life has been consumed by private interests, there is good work for churches to do in recovering the commons in our neighborhoods.

Tim Soerens and his *New Parish* coauthors describe the commons in terms of four interwoven realms: economy, environment, civic participation and education.

The economic realm. The economy undergirds the full commons, the whole shared life of a community. Contrary to popular conceptions, however, the economy is not simply about money. Rather, the authors of *The New Parish* assert that the economy is fundamentally about giving and receiving.[6] Furthermore, they maintain that the work of cultivating the economy of the commons lies largely in imagining and working to establish an economy rooted in abundance and not scarcity. (Scarcity is perhaps *the* fundamental axiom of free-market capitalism.) Our churches need to remind our neighborhoods that God provides abundantly for the care of the whole creation. As a result, there are enough resources for everyone to live and flourish. The challenge, of course, is nurturing relationships in which resources can be given and received such that God's abundant provision can circulate to all neighbors.

As our churches enter into this work of proclaiming, modeling and working toward an economy of abundance, there are many books on themes of abundance and gratitude that could guide us.[7] The theological work of Walter Brueggemann and the community development work of John McKnight and Peter Block (coauthors of the book *The Abundant Community*) point us in this direction, as do reflections on gratitude like Mary Jo Leddy's *Radical Gratitude* and Brother David Steindl-Rast's *Gratefulness: The Heart of Prayer.* Though it is not explicitly faith-based, John McKnight's Asset-Based Community Development Institute offers a multitude of resources that can assist us in working through the practicalities of cultivating an economy rooted in the conviction that God provides abundantly for the flourishing of creation.

The environmental realm. Building on the economic convictions laid out in the previous section, the church should also work to cultivate the environmental realm of the commons. We proclaim to our neighbors that God's abundant provision is integrally connected with the land. Thus we must be attentive to our care of the land and to the ways in which it sustains all our neighbors.

In cultivating the environmental realms of the commons, the church needs to understand how the natural and built environments contribute to and impede flourishing. Reading will help us understand crucial environmental issues that are affecting our place, whether air pollution, an overreliance on automobility, the ways our built environment is short-circuiting human connection or the effects of agribusiness on the land. Reading environmental writers like Wendell Berry, Bill McKibben and Rachel Carson can challenge us to live in ways that reflect better care for the land in our places. The work of theologians and biblical scholars like Norman Wirzba and Ellen Davis is important in helping us articulate the connections between caring for the land in our place and the mission of God in the world.

The educational realm. Another important facet of the commons is our shared responsibility to care for the children of our place. This responsibility is particularly acute in our day, as many children bear the brutal effects of socioeconomic realities related to single-parent families, overwork and failing schools. Reading books that explore these socioeconomic realities, books about the development of children and adolescents, and books on education can help us enter into the work of caring for our children.

A commons approach to education is, as the authors of *The New Parish* point out, much broader than simply caring for our children—although that is of course a crucial element. "Education," they write, "also involves the sharing of local wisdom among neighbors. Learning how to grow heirloom tomatoes from a seasoned gardener, being mentored in the craft of making a rocking chair for your front porch and the like are examples of local wisdom being shared."[8] Churches are well suited not only to curate texts in the traditional way of libraries but also to curate the wisdom of neighbors and to draw on that wisdom by helping people to connect with each other. One church not far from my neighborhood in Indianapolis has hired DeAmon Harges as a "roving listener." Harges's work focuses on listening to neighbors and connecting their wisdom and skills with opportunities in that neighborhood. As a result, neighbors are more connected with one another, and new initiatives are popping up like flowers in the spring. For instance, Harges and his church have helped several neighbors who like to cook to start a catering business. These caterers regularly make meals for events that the church hosts.

The civic realm. The final realm of the commons explored in *The New Parish* is the civic. The civic realm serves to foster laws and institutions that will sustain the work of helping our places to flourish. Reading will help us understand the complexities (and some of the pitfalls) of working in this realm. What are the various laws that give shape to our place, for instance, and to what extent do these laws promote or inhibit the flourishing of our place?

Reading a newspaper or a thoughtful online source of local news and commentary is an essential daily practice as we seek to enter into the work of the civic realm. Occasionally I have the opportunity to teach a class to some homeschoolers in our church. One of the classes that I am currently teaching is on current events. The middle-school students and I are learning to read the newspaper together in order to deepen our understanding of this place in which we live.

The authors of *The New Parish* articulate the civic pressure we all feel to gravitate toward the political ideology of the Right or the Left. The church can bridge this divide as we remember that God is reconciling all humanity in Christ—those on the Right as well as those on the Left. The practice of conversation is crucial to promoting cooperation between Right and Left. Reading books like Sherry Turkle's *Reclaiming Conversation* can help us to understand the virtues of dialogue and to develop practices of conversation in an age in which civil dialogue is a lost art.[9]

Reading is essential to promoting all four facets of the commons. Reading is also an essential practice as we seek to understand where we are and why the culture of our place functions as it does.

As we imagine the flourishing of our place and cultivate its legacy, the practice of reading will draw us deeper into the shared life of our neighborhood. The transformative power of reading, however, is not limited to our neighborhoods; it can also promote the flourishing of the wider world—the subject of the next two chapters.

seven

Hope for Our
Interconnected Creation

[The Church] is the possibility given to man to see in and through
this world the "world to come," to see it and to live it in Christ.
. . . A Christian is the one who, wherever he looks, finds Christ
and rejoices in Him. And this joy transforms all his human plans
and programs, decisions and actions, making all his mission the
sacrament of the world's return to Him who is the life of the world.

ALEXANDER SCHMEMANN

W endell Berry is one of my favorite living poets. I am especially fond of his sabbath poems, which he writes
during Sunday walks through a wooded area on his Kentucky
farm. The sabbath poems reflect many of the themes Berry has
explored in his novels, short stories, essays and other poetry—
nature, land, community and place.

Perhaps my favorite sabbath poem is one Berry wrote in
2007, a poem about hope. Berry observes that hope is hard to
come by because the course of Western culture has led to the

looting and polluting of forests, fields, streams and mountains. At the end of this road is only more destruction; we must have the courage to imagine a different way. Berry's poem suggests one way toward hope: "Hope then / to belong to your place by your own knowledge / of what it is that no other place is, and by / your caring for it as you care for no other place."[1]

As the poem unfolds, Berry fleshes out a vision of the flourishing of a place. What is striking to me is that while the flourishing of the local is undoubtedly primary for Berry, he concludes the poem with a suggestion of how the world at large might be redeemed. Using our imagination, we see that other people in other places have similar struggles, and we should care about whether they get to pursue flourishing in their place too. In an interconnected creation, we cannot separate the health and flourishing of our place from the health and flourishing of all places. In a passage in his essay "It All Turns on Affection" that parallels the final stanzas of this poem, Berry describes the connection between our places and the world:

> For humans to have a responsible relationship to the world, they must imagine their places in it. . . . By imagination, we recognize with sympathy the fellow members, human and nonhuman, with whom we share our place. By that local experience we see the need to grant a sort of preemptive sympathy to all the fellow members, the neighbors, with whom we share the world. As imagination enables sympathy, sympathy enables affection. And in affection we find the possibility of a neighborly, kind and conserving [world].[2]

REIMAGINING THE WORLD

The work of imagining the world in new ways is essential to our bearing witness to God's transforming work. The new creation that God is bringing forth stands in contrast to the status quo of the world's prevailing powers. In order to act faithfully within the story of God's bringing healing and flourishing to the world, we must begin to imagine and understand the world in new and deeper ways.

The reality that at times we will have to overhaul our basic understanding of the world is fundamental to our identity as learning organizations. As an essential first step, we will have to reimagine the very structure and nature of the world. As ones who have been deeply formed by the powers of modernity, we have inherited a fragmented, individualistic understanding of the world. We see people and other entities not as fellow creatures to whom we are inextricably connected but rather as atoms—isolated units that occasionally interact with one another. Most of our social and legal theory in Western culture has been built on the basic conviction of a fragmented world.

Reimagining the world is a massive task, too large for any one individual or one lifetime. Our imagination of the world will change only slowly and gradually, over many centuries and with the contributions of a vast host of faithful thinkers. The joy of finding Christ everywhere we look in his wondrous creation, as Schmemann observes in the epigraph above, is a sort of leaven that works its way into our minds, transforming the ways we envision the world. Just as reading can guide us deeper into our understanding of who we are as churches and of the places where we live, it can also help us begin to grasp the ways in which we are connected to people in other places. Reading illuminates and deepens our bonds with others—our fraternal bonds with other churches; our ecological bonds with those who live in the same watershed or region; and our geopolitical bonds with those who live in the same city, state, province or nation.

We do not imagine, or reimagine, the world in a vacuum. Modern approaches to reimagining or transforming the world tend to be "trickle-down" strategies. These methods work from the conviction that if we can develop a perfect socioeconomic philosophy that is relevant to the most powerful parts of the world—if not the entire world—everything else fall into place within the system. This tendency is perhaps illustrated most vividly in a presidential election year, when the public conversation is dominated by the quest for the Oval Office. Our obsession with presidential politics unmasks our conviction that many of our problems will be solved if we could only get the right person into that office. Unfortunately, such approaches consistently fail because—given the finitude of human reasoning—they inevitably oversimplify the world. No perfect candidates exist, and we cannot develop a perfect political or economic system. We will inevitably misrepresent the world. Our theories cannot adequately represent all people and places within it. Instead we should try to grapple with and reimagine the world from the grassroots up—expanding outward from the particular places and communities in which we live and work. To the extent that we are faithful within our church communities and neighborhoods as they begin to flourish, we will be able to begin to reimagine the world in ways that move us in the direction of its flourishing.

AN INTERCONNECTED CREATION

If we follow the wisdom of the Berry poem examined above, our churches should be primarily concerned with belonging well to our places and caring deeply for them. But my neighborhood is integrally connected with yours. The work of the local church—as it relates to other local places—centers on equipping others in those places to pursue *shalom* there and on the cultivation of regional, national and global systems that foster the flourishing of all places. We cannot work toward the flourishing of some people or places at the expense of others. The great injustice of colonialism, for example, was that it sought the flourishing of European peoples at the immense expense of the lives and freedom of native peoples in the Americas, Africa and other colonial regions.

Reading is vital to the task of understanding our interconnected creation and the natural and socioeconomic bonds that hold our places together. Although we have been formed by Western culture to think of the world in terms of fragmented atoms, contemporary physics is uncovering a deeper reality. Reading works of contemporary physics, chaos theory or ecology can help loosen the grip of our assumptions about the fragmented nature of creation. It can also expand our understanding of the various relationships that tie us together in God's creation: for example, geographic relationships (creatures living in proximity to one another) or dietary relationships (creatures eating creatures).

Poets have a keen way of illuminating the bonds of creation in ways that might never have occurred to us. The work of Ernesto Cardenal, with its poignant themes of the interconnectedness of creation, has captivated my imagination. One of the most heralded poets of Nicaragua, Cardenal was a close friend of Thomas Merton. For Cardenal, the rich biology that he encounters in his native land is tightly woven with the stars and the celestial fabric of creation. "The egg of life / is one," he writes, "from / the first bubble of gas, to the iguana's egg, to the New Man."[3]

We have been formed by the powers of the modern age to start from the assumption of a fragmented world, but the biblical writers were not working from this assumption. Theologian Howard Snyder has observed that Scripture is undergirded by the opposite conviction, that creation is an interconnected whole:

In an ecological understanding, everything is related to everything else. The study of ecosystems helps us grasp the nature of these interrelationships and learn how to work for stable and flourishing systems, overcoming the maladies that harm or even destroy an ecosystem over time. . . . [This] ecological conception is biblical at heart and can be an important tool in helping us understand the comprehensive healing message of the gospel.[4]

All followers of Christ today should have some sense of the interconnectedness of creation and of its significance for the shape of our life together in Christ. It is relatively easy to energize people in our churches and neighborhoods to care for their own corner of the globe. It is much more challenging to get people to care deeply about the health and flourishing of distant places. A basic theological understanding of ecology can be an important first step toward understanding why concerns like violence in the Middle East or the poaching of wildlife in Africa matter to us at home in North America.

READING TO DEEPEN THE BONDS BETWEEN CHURCHES

We need to be attentive to the bonds that link us to people in other places and to the work of deepening these bonds. Reading is a vital tool in this process of linking ourselves to other places. As followers of Jesus, our primary connection is with others— and particularly other churches—to whom we have been united in Jesus' death, burial, resurrection and ascension. Although we have been united in Christ, this unification has yet to be fully realized. As we yearn for the fullness of unity, our main work lies in challenging each other to deeper faithfulness.

At the roots of the Christian tradition lie the churches of the first and second centuries, which were connected in large part by writing, reading and sharing letters. Many early churches read and shared the letters of the apostle Paul that were eventually collected in the New Testament. Other letters and writings that were not included in the canon of Scripture were also shared among churches. Reading epistles was an important way that churches found out about and entered into the situations of their sister congregations. Paul's pleas for the churches in Rome and Corinth to support the church in Jerusalem, for instance, were undoubtedly read and discerned in other churches as well. This tradition of connecting to other churches through reading and writing should guide our imaginations as we think about cultivating deeper relationships between churches in the twenty-first century.

It is beneficial for us to link with churches based on both affinity and diversity. Affinities might include denomination (or other historical tradition), setting (urban, suburban, rural) and vocation (the sort of work in which we are involved, including community development, arts, education, childcare, etc.). Although affinity links often come naturally, the challenge is to deepen these relationships, encouraging one another across the distance.

Linking by diversity comes less naturally to us, but it is just as vital. The authors of *The New Parish* write:

> Forming bonds across diverse places can expand your capacity for solidarity and collaboration. Intentionally developing relationships with communities that are culturally different than your own parish forms you as a [people] who can delight in the rich diversity of God's creation. The cultural biases and blind spots that all humans naturally develop over the course of generations are confronted by experiencing other ways of doing things.[5]

The Shalom Mission Communities (SMC) is an association of intentional Christian communities spread across the United

States. For almost twenty-five years these communities have nurtured a relationship with Valle Nuevo, "a campesino village of repatriated refugees in El Salvador." People from these communities regularly visit Valle Nuevo and vice versa. "Valle Nuevo," SMC states, has helped us "understand Jesus's presence in the poor who are rich in faith."[6] This cross-cultural relationship is a wonderful example of linking across diversity and a powerful reminder that such links are most beneficial when sustained over a long period of time, not simply occasional events over a short season.

Reading can substantially enrich the work of linking, as it did for churches in the early centuries. Recommending books to churches with whom we have affinity can tighten the bonds of that affinity. We can share resources that have helped us grow deeper in our tradition or denomination, as well as resources that have helped us better understand and embody what it means to be a church in our particular setting.

We can also share resources in order to help us understand and appreciate our differences. Reading can help us to understand one another's experiences and to incite conversation. A predominantly white church might read a book like Michelle Alexander's *The New Jim Crow* and discuss it with a predominantly African American church, listening attentively to how the latter church's experiences line up (or don't line up) with what they have read.

READING TO DEEPEN OUR ECOLOGICAL BONDS

Beyond the links we share with other churches, perhaps our next most significant link is the ecological bonds that link us in the order of creation with others who live near us. These ecological bonds consist largely of basic natural resources that we share in common, including soil, air and water.

All too often we take the soil underneath our feet for granted, but it is this very soil that is the lifeblood of our food economy.

Plants of course need soil to grow, and most animals that we eat thrive on a diet consisting largely of plants. Even in nonagricultural areas, such as cities, soil health is essential to human health and flourishing. In my Indianapolis neighborhood there are many parcels of land that are unusable brownfields, in which the soil has been contaminated by previous generations. One neighbor who lives down my street and adjacent to a brownfield was plagued with cancer. The disease was believed to have originated from gases and polluted water that seeped into her home from the brownfield. The contaminated soil of brownfields can be remediated, as the one adjacent to my neighbor's home has been, but only at great cost, and sometimes the cost is so astronomical as to render the damage irreversible. A parcel of urban land, for instance, can be certified as safe for human habitation although the groundwater is not safe for human use.

We cannot continue to take the soil for granted. We need a deeper understanding of how it binds us to people in other times and other places, as well as how to care well for the soil we inhabit. Reading is an essential part of this work of understanding and caring for the soil. Many books have been written on soil as a vital part of human flourishing, from kids' books like *Dirt: The Scoop on Soil* to very detailed biological and chemical studies. For a basic introduction to soil intended for adults, I usually recommend Gene Logsdon's *The Gardener's Guide to Better Soil* and his related book *Holy Shit: Managing Manure to Save Mankind*. If you want a theological exploration of why soil matters, I recommend starting with Ragan Sutterfield's *Cultivating Reality: How the Soil Might Save Us*. Beyond such introductory books, it would benefit our churches and neighborhoods for some scientifically inclined readers in our congregations to study how contaminated soil can be remediated and brought back to health.

Similar explorations are in order as we seek to understand the air that we breathe. Just as our soil is prone to pollution, our air is prone to its own forms of contamination. In many urban areas, smog is one sort of air pollution whose effects are felt across many neighborhoods. In areas that have a coal-fired power plant or high levels of automobile traffic, pollution from these sources contributes significantly to poor air quality. We would do well to understand the habits that contribute to air pollution, from automobile use to industrial pollution to use of electricity from coal-fired plants—and, of course, begin to develop new habits that generate less pollution. Many books have been written at all levels on air pollution; a good introduction for adults is Hans Tammemagi's *Air: Our Planet's Ailing Atmosphere.*

As we learn about soil and air quality, we also should learn about our water supply. A fitting place to begin such explorations is with our water bill and learning more about the agency that pipes water into our house. In order to understand the economics of water, we need to read about our watershed, the ecological regions that are bound together by their shared waterways. What is your watershed? What other communities share it? What bodies of water—rivers, creeks, lakes—does it contain? What types of pollution threaten the health and vitality of your water? What are the sources of this pollution? What economic or political activity, if any, is already under way to address these sources of pollution, and how can you be involved? Reading, again, is the primary way that we begin to tackle these questions.

Ched Myers, a well-known theologian, has been advocating in recent years for "watershed discipleship," a practical way forward for churches that want to be attentive to their region's people, land, creatures and certainly water. Myers writes:

To be faithful disciples *in* a watershed at this watershed historical moment, . . . we need to become disciples *of* our watersheds, which have everything to teach us about interrelatedness and resiliency. This requires literacy; to paraphrase Baba Dioum, a Senegalese environmentalist:

• We won't save places we don't love.

• We can't love places we don't know.

• And we don't know places we haven't learned.[7]

As we grow in knowledge of the environmental resources that connect us to other places, we are drawn closer to the people and the places with whom we share these vital resources.

READING TO DEEPEN OUR GEOPOLITICAL BONDS

Regardless of where we live, our place is located within a hierarchy of geopolitical regions. We likely belong to a town or city, a county, a state or province and a nation. Within each of these geopolitical regions, we are bound together with its other residents. If we live in a city, our neighborhood is geopolitically bound to other neighborhoods that make up the city. If we live in a rural town, we are bound together with other towns that are part of our county. Cities and counties are bound together as part of a state (or province), and states/provinces are bound together as part of a nation. These sorts of connections are very familiar to us; they are fundamental to the way that we learn to talk about the world at a very young age. And yet we often take these bonds for granted and don't reflect much on what it means to belong to a city or a state and what it might look like for our city or state to flourish.

Certainly each geopolitical region has economic and governmental systems that define it to a large degree. We will explore these systems in more detail in the next chapter. A region, however, is not defined solely by its economy or its politics. There are many other institutions that are shared across a region and that contribute significantly to the shape of life in that part of the world. A wide range of educational systems—from preschools to universities—are shared and operated within geopolitical regions. School systems are often tied most closely with a county or city, but they also typically operate within the governance of statewide and nationwide educational systems. Much of our infrastructure—roads, utilities and the like—are shared and operated within a certain geopolitical area. A particular region will likely have its own distinctive calendar. Here in Indianapolis, the month of May is widely associated with cultural events tied to the Indianapolis 500 race at the end of that month. In many rural regions, the county fair marks an important season of the year that gives shape to life in that area. A region will also have a unique history that narrates its development.

Reading is an important means for us to understand the bonds that link us with other places within our geopolitical region. Through reading we can learn more about the history, the economy, the schools and the culture of our county, our state or our nation. Our aim in reading in these sorts of ways is not mere accumulation of knowledge but rather the sort of understanding that allows us to be engaged in meaningful, redemptive ways in the transformation of these regions. In order to imagine the flourishing of creation as a whole, we need to cultivate deeper understandings of our connection with people in other places and begin to live in ways that demonstrate that these connections matter. Reading about the bonds that connect us with other places is vital to the journey out of autonomy and into a more integrated way of life that seeks the flourishing of all places.

This journey toward flourishing requires not only that we become increasingly familiar with those to whom we are connected but also that we begin to reimagine the sorts of economic and political bonds that tie our place to others. In the next chapter we will focus on these two kinds of bonds and how reading can help us to imagine them in new and more Christlike ways.

eight
. . . . . .

Toward Faithful Engagement
in Economics and Politics

The novelist with Christian concerns will find in modern
life distortions which are repugnant to him, and his
problem will be to make these appear as distortions to
an audience which is used to seeing them as natural.

FLANNERY O'CONNOR

F orty years ago Englewood Christian Church, my church
community, was like a lot of other large evangelical
churches. We were not involved in economics or politics as a
congregation beyond the scope of our life together and the participation of our members as individuals. While today we aren't
exactly super-active in politics or economics beyond our neighborhood, we are definitely more engaged in these arenas than
we have been in previous generations. This shift follows from
our efforts in getting to know our neighborhood and working
with our neighbors toward its flourishing, as well as maturing

in our understanding of the ways that our neighborhood is connected to other places.

Our involvement in broader economic and political issues has flowed from the work that we are doing as a church in our neighborhood—particularly in early childhood education and community development. Doing either of these kinds of work well will inevitably lead to collaboration with the governmental organizations that oversee it. It will also lead to participation in refining legislation that helps the work to be done in ways that promote the flourishing of people and neighborhoods. In our early childhood education work, we have taken a stand with state legislators and others calling for making quality preschool education available to all children and for statewide economic legislation that would fund such an initiative. After a couple of tragic incidents here in Indiana, including one in which a young child at a church-based daycare center drowned in a baptistery, we have also pushed for stricter legislation that would promote the safety and learning of young children in other church daycares.

In our community development work, we have worked closely for many years with the city's Department of Metropolitan Development, which funds and oversees community development projects across the city. Some of the affordable housing that we have created and managed has been funded through federal housing programs. As food access has been a particular challenge for our neighborhood, we also have done a substantial amount of work on this issue both within our neighborhood and in partnership with state and national groups. For instance, we have recently partnered with a company based in Toledo, Ohio, to start a hydroponic growing operation. This initiative has required working not only with this corporation but also with a range of other partners and funders at the city, state and national levels.

In the last few years we have been working diligently to promote the use of solar energy in our neighborhood and beyond, an effort that includes installing solar panels on the roof of our church building. One of the challenges that we have encountered in these efforts was that the coal industry was lobbying for state legislation that would make it difficult for families and corporations to install and use solar panels. This proposed legislation was not in the interest of healthy neighborhoods or of creation as a whole. Working with environmental groups and others who opposed it, we were able to stall it indefinitely.

Our church has not entered into broader economic or political arenas on the basis of abstract issues that we feel strongly about but rather as extensions of the work of knowing and loving our place, as described over the last three chapters. Reading has been vital to this journey, helping us understand the arenas that we are working in and the issues that we are engaging.

Literature, especially fiction and poetry, can be immensely helpful to us in the work delineated in the previous five chapters: imagining a shared life that is rooted in knowledge of ourselves and our places and in the connections we have with people in other places. Literature is not as helpful in the more abstract work of imagining what healthy economies and politics look like in broad arenas like states and nations. Some modern poets and novelists are writing excellent works that are deeply political, but their politics almost always takes a negative approach: telling us what healthy, flourishing societies are *not* instead of what they are. Allen Ginsberg, for instance, rages in his poem "America": "America I've given you all and now I'm nothing. . . . America when will we end the human war?"[1] The poet Steve Mason likewise, in writing critically about his experiences as a soldier in Vietnam, makes a bold statement that warmongering societies are not healthy ones. Dystopian novels like George Orwell's *1984* and

Aldous Huxley's *Brave New World* also take a negative approach, vividly depicting what healthy societies are *not*.

Literature excels in depicting particularities. It does not fare so well in grappling with the abstractions needed to order society at large. "Poetry hates the generality," writes Clyde Kilby in *Poetry and Life*, "not because the generality is untrue but because the generality is unconvincing."[2] Similarly, fiction excels at telling specific stories of particular people and places.

One of the clearest arguments that writers (and especially Christian writers) serve their society best by writing in a negative mode is Flannery O'Connor's essay "The Fiction Writer and His Country." Responding to an editorial in *Life* magazine that griped that no novelist spoke for America, O'Connor makes the case that the fiction writer speaks best for her country when she critiques its imperfections. "My own feeling," she writes, "is that writers who see by the light of their Christian faith will have, in these times, the sharpest eyes for the grotesque, for the perverse and for the unacceptable."[3] This essay, I believe, offers some of the keenest wisdom for how churches should be involved in economics and politics beyond the local arena. Our primary objective is not to foist a vision of flourishing upon society but rather to name in a clear and unwavering way that which is unacceptable in society and to demand that it be addressed.

REIMAGINING ECONOMICS

Following O'Connor's lead as we seek to engage faithfully in the economic systems of our day, we must recognize that the domination of transnational corporations in our globalized economy impedes the flourishing of many places and indeed the flourishing of the world as a whole. Our work begins, then, with reimagining the nature of economics, or at least changing the perspective from which we understand economics. Our economic imaginations in the twenty-first century have been deeply formed by the forces of globalization. Most of us are surrounded by globalization whenever we go out of our home. The landscape is dotted with retail outposts of transnational corporations. Even very small towns often have at least one fast food restaurant or a gas station branded by a major oil company. We tend to think of cities as the hubs of globalization, but many rural areas are also saturated with the branding for transnational companies—for example, agriculture brands in farming regions. Even our online experience is dominated by transnational corporations: from the hardware and software that we utilize to our preferred search engines to the various social media platforms that we frequent.

Because the economy of globalization is so pervasive in the twenty-first century, it is important for our churches to understand globalization and its impact. Walter Brueggemann has noted that the two primary functions of the prophetic imagination are criticism and energizing. In order for us to offer a compelling critique of globalization, we need to have a deep understanding of it. Cultivating this sort of deep understanding will be impossible without reading. Careful, attentive reading can help us navigate complex questions about globalization. How did we come to be so saturated by the global economy? What forces are driving it? Can these forces be reversed, and at what cost? What places does the global economy help to flourish, and in what places does it inhibit flourishing? We should especially be attentive to the voices of those who are being excluded from the global economy or those who are suffering as a result of it. For instance, we should pay attention to those who have lost their jobs when cheaper labor was found in another corner of the world, or those whose land and health have been wrecked by transnational corporations.

In order to imagine and energize alternative economies, we need a different entry point into the conversation. Economics, at its most basic level, is about livelihood: How do we sustain our neighbors and ourselves and provide the basic resources necessary for life and well-being? Perhaps we should begin, then, not in the abstract realm, with models of micro- or macroeconomics, but with the basic needs we all share: food, clothing and shelter. How do the people at home and elsewhere secure these resources? Where do the food that we eat and the water that we drink come from? the clothes we wear? the materials to build our homes? How are these resources transported from other communities to our own, and at what cost? How do other communities rely on ours for food and resources? Reading is a crucial part of finding the answers to these questions that illuminate our economies.

Let's start at the grocery store. We might not think of the grocery store as a place where we might read, beyond perhaps comparing price tags. But take a notebook with you next time you go to the grocery store, and start reading the labels on some essential food items and taking notes. What are the ingredients? Where was the food grown or manufactured? Most food labels include the producer's web address. Go online to learn more about where the food came from and how it got to your grocer's shelf. Search the Internet to see what you can find about the company that produced it. What are other people saying about it? Has this company been in the news, and why? You will find that some global food brands are quite controversial. How are these companies perceived in the places where they operate, especially in developing countries?

Generally, it is beneficial to tighten the radius of where our food comes from, eating as locally as possible. This sort of diet not only reduces the amount of energy needed to bring the food to our table. It also is an investment in the region where we are most likely to have other ecological, economic or cultural bonds. Not only do we get the benefit of buying food from our neighbors, but our purchases contribute to the tax base there. These taxes help to fund services that benefit some of the most vulnerable people in our areas.

But distance shouldn't be the only factor that we consider in choosing our food. If some of our food is coming from a conflict region, what is the connection between our food and the conflict? Reading and research are the primary tools we have to begin answering these complex, sometimes difficult questions. As we try to understand the food economy, there are many books that can shed light on the agricultural situation of our times. A few useful books include Michael Pollen's *The Omnivore's Dilemma*, Wendell Berry's *The Unsettling of America* and Eric Schlosser's *Fast Food Nation*.

Many questions similar to those that have been asked here about food could also be asked about our water (as discussed in chapter seven), our clothing and the materials we use to build or maintain our homes. All of the reading and research required to live thoughtful, intentional, deeply rooted yet broadly linked lives may seem overwhelming at first. But when we approach this work not as individuals but as a church community, it won't seem quite so burdensome. People will be passionate about different topics. The biggest challenge is creating spaces in which people can share about what they are reading and then discuss and discern together how their learnings might affect the shared life of the church. This challenge is fundamental to all learning organizations, as described by Peter Senge. How do we bring together our reading and learning and allow it to transform the ways that we live and act as a people? Maybe the church will decide not to buy certain products or recommend that members not buy certain things. On the flipside, a church could recommend buying from certain local farmers or retailers. On the basis of its collective reading, a church might decide to host a seminar on how to conserve water or energy resources. Such a seminar might also include some theological discussion of why such resources should be conserved.

Reading alone will not transform our communities. It is in dialogue and discernment that we are challenged and commit ourselves to the practices (economic and otherwise) that will change us.

Toward Faithful Politics

At its best, politics is about cultivating the common good of the *polis*—a Greek word that literally means city but can also mean region. *Politics* is another name for the systems and structures that we use to protect and expand the commons, not just in our own place, as discussed in chapter six, but throughout a city, state, province or nation. Just as our economic imaginations have been saturated with globalization, our political imaginations are rife with varying conceptions of democracy. Democratic government—at least in theory—has much to commend it. However, Western democracies in practice generally fall far short of the ideal.

Following Flannery O'Connor's recommendation that we name the unacceptable realities in our society, we should be clear that democratic systems have always tended to work in favor of the wealthy. In the twenty-first century we see this tendency most clearly in the lobbying efforts of industries and corporations and the sway that they hold over every level of politics. In our day cultivating the common good for *everyone* often takes a backseat to divergent partisan visions of how best to move in that direction.

Working from this historical observation that democratic societies tend to favor the wealthy and the powerful, we would do well to name this bias, to work against it and to advocate for those who are neither wealthy nor powerful. Following in the vein of O'Connor's assertion that the best writing is a critique of society at large, Robert Penn Warren's novel *All The King's Men* offers us a timely vision of the ways in which politics tends to be corrupted by money and power. So one particular way we could become engaged is to work toward limits and transparency in the efforts of special interest groups to contribute to campaigns and sway politicians.

For over a decade I have been involved with the Christian Community Development Association (CCDA), which has found some degree of success in advocating for communities that are neither wealthy nor powerful. CCDA was founded in the late 1980s by renowned civil rights activist John Perkins. The political history of CCDA is a good illustration of the political strategy that I sketched above. CCDA's primary work has always been supporting and connecting faith-based groups who are working toward the flourishing of their particular places. However, after over a decade of doing this work, CCDA realized that there were certain issues that affected many of the neighborhoods in which their members were working: for instance, immigration issues, education issues and pollution issues. They also realized that by drawing on their network they could have substantial influence in advocacy related to some of these issues. "For years, CCDA has said [that] the path to building healthy and sustainable neighborhoods is doing church there as well as doing compassion and development work," notes CEO Noel Castellanos, "but there was another element missing: the confrontation of injustice."[4]

By mobilizing its network, CCDA found that it has had significant political clout to resist injustice. CCDA has had some successes in recent years in advocating for education reform and immigration reform. "We weren't looking for issues to get involved in," says Castellanos; "we were simply looking at [the systemic challenges] facing our neighborhoods."[5] As CCDA's story illustrates, our political strategy *beyond* our neighborhoods should flow from the work we are doing *inside* our neighborhoods.

READING AND POLITICAL ACTION

Reading is essential to political engagement, whether that involves voting, signing petitions, initiating public forums or building alliances. Reading is particularly important when we wade into the legislative process. In order to engage well with the changing of old laws or the writing of new ones, we need to have *read* the laws: existing ones, proposed ones and amendments. A friend who has worked with the Indiana state legislature recently told me that the pace of legislation is such that even many legislators regularly vote on bills that they have not had time to read thoroughly. Partisan tactics often exacerbate this problem, as the party who is driving a particular bill might give its own party ample time to read the bill but delay providing it to the opposing party until the very last possible second.

Can we fight for legislative structures and policy that would slow the pace of this work enough to allow all legislators to read and reflect on a given bill before voting on it, and also allow citizens and groups outside the legislature to read and comment on the legislation? Fast legislation cannot work in favor of the common good of all constituents.

Understanding and participating in the legislative process will help prepare us to critique it. As we do so, it is beneficial for us not only to read existing and proposed bills but also to read commentary about proposed changes: Who supports or opposes the changes, and what is their rationale for doing so? Because our political imagination has been shaped to such a large degree by voting, we may also need to remind ourselves of how the complete civic process works and how we can be faithfully involved in it.

As illustrated in the story at the beginning of this chapter, our political action as churches should be guided by the work we are already engaged in as church communities. That work should take precedence over the politics, but sometimes policy will impede our work or even contribute to the systems we are trying to reform. In these cases we may need to get engaged to help remove (or minimize the effect of) unjust policies. For example, if we have members of our church or neighbors who are immigrants, or if we have partner churches that are composed largely of immigrants, we should be attentive to immigration policy. If we have farmers, ranchers or gardeners in our congregation, or others who are involved in food production, we should carefully watch food policy.

There also are areas of policy that should not escape our notice even if they are not directly related to our day-to-day life and work. I'm thinking particularly here of issues that have a major impact on the life and well-being of people in other places in our nation and around the globe. We should be attentive to military policies, as they have extensive ramifications for people in nations that are under siege by our military. Additionally, as a large body of research has demonstrated in recent years, our military policy is a powerful contributor to posttraumatic stress disorder and other mental health issues among our nation's own veterans. We need to be attentive to environmental policy regarding issues like pollution and climate change, as often those who feel the effects of our policies most deeply are those in poverty-stricken areas or developing nations. Similarly, we should be attentive to abortion policy, as the unborn are a vulnerable people who are not able to represent themselves. These areas of policy concern matters of life and death, and as long as we ignore them, the whole of creation will not be able to flourish.

Reading, of course, can help us to engage a wide range of policies in meaningful and helpful ways. To be engaged in the world in transformative ways, we must understand the history of an issue or a particular policy position. We can ask: What are the forces that have driven this policy to develop into its present form? If we perceive threats to legislation that we believe is beneficial, who are the parties behind these threats, why are they challenging the laws, and how can we best engage them? Without a robust commitment to reading, we are perhaps more likely to stereotype the opposition, assume the worst of them and make sure that the answers we find only confirm those assumptions.

READING AND VOTING

Although other types of political activity are arguably more effective in promoting the common good, voting is an important political activity in a democratic society. Important as it may be, the practice of voting does need to be reimagined. In the US popular imagination, voting is dominated by the two-party system, and voters are encouraged to be loyal to their particular party. Perhaps one of the most significant ways in which we can reimagine voting is to refuse to be pawns of a political party. For each race let us choose the candidate, regardless of party, who we believe will best promote the health and flourishing of his or her jurisdiction. Broadcast media thrives on partisan politics; to truly vote independently, we will have to do a significant amount of reading and research. Broadcast media coverage of the electoral process also is largely confined to soundbites, especially in "low-profile" races. Reading is essential to understanding the platforms of particular candidates—not only what that candidate stands for and why but also who is bankrolling his or her campaign. We are tempted to reduce politics to talking points and soundbites and basic emotional responses. Reading helps us to resist this temptation. It helps us cultivate the common good in more informed ways. Amassing a deep and truly non-partisan knowledge of the candidates is a much better use of our time than tracking the horserace through polls or living and dying on primary returns.

And I can't avoid mentioning referenda and ballot initiatives here. A referendum may be abstruse even after we have read it, but it is impossible to understand if we don't read it at all. By reading a referendum and some commentary on it, we can arrive at an educated rationale for a vote for or against it. Then we can also work to educate other voters in our church and neighborhood on why it is important to vote in a particular way on that item.

The last six chapters have presented a detailed case for the importance of reading to the flourishing of our churches, neighborhoods and world. But in a culture in which careful reading is a rare art, how do we cultivate the habits of this art in our local church congregations? This question will be the focus of the next chapter.

nine

Becoming a Reading Congregation

Love itself is knowledge:
the more one loves, the more one knows.

ATTRIBUTED TO ST. GREGORY THE GREAT

How we can promote the practice of reading in our churches so that it becomes embedded in our congregational DNA? Ultimately this challenge hinges on the thought expressed above by St. Gregory: Do we love God, our neighbors and the world? If we answer in the affirmative, we demonstrate that love by seeking to know God and the world. We might vigorously pursue this knowledge in a host of different ways. In the text-saturated culture of the twenty-first century, however, reading is an essential tool that we will need to use well.

LEARNING TO READ SLOWLY

The first and absolutely essential step in the journey toward becoming a reading congregation is to encourage and practice the slow, attentive reading of Scripture. If we cannot read Scripture carefully and well, it is doubtful we will be able to do so with other books. When I talk about reading Scripture, I am not thinking of private devotional reading. Rather, I have in mind habits of shared reading that shape the common life of our church communities. To know the scriptural story in intimate ways is to grow deeper in our love for this story in which we are enmeshed.

Earlier in this book the practices of lectio divina (chapter one) and "reading in communion" (chapter three) were discussed. If you want your church to start the journey toward a deeper, more transformative knowledge of the scriptural story, introduce them to these practices. Small groups or Sunday school classes, for instance, might read and discuss Stephen Fowl and Gregory Jones's *Reading in Communion* or one of the excellent books on lectio divina. If you are a pastor with preaching responsibilities, you could craft a sermon series on *how* we read Scripture, introducing both of these practices. Another option might be to offer a special workshop on how to read Scripture carefully and in communion. Whatever the preferred educational format of your congregation, a conversation on reading Scripture will be beneficial to promote deeper practices of reading. Find ways to get your congregation thinking and talking about what is happening during the sermon. Discuss how it can be a more engaged time of reading and reflection for the whole congregation.

READING THROUGHOUT OUR SHARED LIFE

Beyond the practice of reading Scripture, find ways to connect reading to as many church activities as possible. Does your church have a charity ministry that gives out food, clothing or other assistance? Or are you involved with a homeless shelter or other parachurch group that does this kind of work? Encourage the people involved in that work to read a book like *When Helping Hurts*, by Steve Corbett and Brian Fikkert, that will challenge and inspire them. Does your church have a pre-school or school? Encourage the teachers to read and discuss books on teaching, child development or equity in education. Find opportunities for them to discuss what they are reading—at least with other teachers. Encourage the people who work with the children or youth of your church to read and discuss a book relevant to this work. Even reading just one book a year in conjunction with others who are doing similar ministry, and hosting a single meeting to discuss the book, would promote the practices of reading and conversation in very practical ways.

One caveat is in order here about promoting the practice of reading across the whole church community: expect, and accept, diversity. Not everyone is capable of or willing to read the latest and thickest theology tome. Want to recommend books to accompany a sermon series? Try recommending several books on the theme that will connect with people at different levels of education, different preferences and differing amounts of available time. If possible, include a relevant fiction book with your recommendations.

As congregational leaders hoping to promote reading as a spiritual practice, you will have to learn the nuances of challenging and stretching church members without overwhelming them or turning them off completely to the idea. At Englewood Christian Church we've read some pretty intense books as a congregation. Some of these books, such as Gerhard Lohfink's *Jesus and Community* or Jonathan Bonk's *Missions and Money*, aren't often read outside a seminary classroom. But we didn't just jump right into them. We read other books that prepared us. And although many people did read these books, not everyone joined in. Church members should never be coerced into reading a particular book.

CREATING A CONVERSATIONAL SPACE

As we seek to become a reading congregation, it's not enough to read books; we need to talk about them with others. Reading and conversation go hand in hand. I doubt it is possible to promote the practice of reading without having a space in which to discuss books. It is in conversation that we make connections between what we read and how we live. It is through these connections that books endear themselves to us. In conversation we are also energized to dive even deeper into reading. Although many types of conversational spaces are possible for our churches, I will suggest four general types here.

First, look at the spaces in which you are already having conversations. Explore new ways in which you could integrate books as parts of these conversations. These spaces might include Sunday school classes, small groups, staff meetings and meetings of ministry teams. If Sunday school classes or small groups focus primarily on reading Scripture together, perhaps a relevant book or commentary could be interwoven with the biblical study. Although we don't have a small groups program at Englewood, we do have small groups that meet for a season to read and discuss a section of Scripture or a particular book. When a group in our church plans to read Scripture, a handful of commentaries and other resources are usually recommended to help illuminate the biblical text.

In addition to promoting reading in existing spaces, consider creating new conversation spaces. Host workshops or seminars for church members, neighbors or other churches. Plan a seminar on a book or a topic. Invite those who want to take part to read the book(s) beforehand. Spend an afternoon or evening discussing the book or topic. Perhaps you have an author in your congregation or neighborhood: invite her to lead a conversation about her latest book. I know firsthand that authors often travel to promote a recent book. They are often on the lookout for churches that will host a conversation.

A more informal type of conversational space is a book club. Some churches have started book clubs for their members or for neighbors. Book clubs are a great way to read and discuss fiction or thematic books (say a gardening book club or a contemporary philosophy book club). Thematic book clubs in particular are a great way to engage neighbors. Coffee shops, libraries and bookstores are often more than willing to host these groups. Although I generally recommend that churches extend hospitality to neighbors, it might be most hospitable to host a book group off site (some neighbors might be hesitant to attend a book club that meets in a church).

A book review is more formal than a book club, but it can also generate conversation. A book review not only introduces a book but is a way of talking about and reflecting on the book's content. Devote part of your church website or newsletter to occasional book reviews penned by members who love to read and write. My church has taken this to the next level. Eight years ago we started the *Englewood Review of Books* (*ERB*) website. Two years later we would launch a quarterly print edition of the *ERB*. Thousands of people read the *ERB* every month, and it pays a portion of my salary. Creative churches may also find ways to curate reviews that members have written on their personal blogs. Website comments, if carefully monitored, can generate conversations among church members, fostering something deeper than one person's take on a book.

MAKING BOOKS AND RESOURCES ACCESSIBLE

A related challenge is the question of how to make good and pertinent books and resources accessible to the congregation. Typically, when churches want to make books accessible, they do so through either a library or a bookstore. Churches that have their own bookstores tend to be larger, as a bookstore requires personnel who can keep up with inventory and finances. But small churches can have bookstores too. When I came to Englewood over a decade ago, it was a small church of no more than 150 people. Yet it had a bookstore. Perhaps calling it a store is an overstatement, but the church did keep several shelves stocked with recommended books for reading and discussion. The church made these books available at cost to members, visitors and neighbors.

Englewood's story is a great illustration of how a bookstore does not necessarily require exorbitant amounts of space, money or personnel. If you think a bookstore would benefit your congregation but don't have the resources to sustain it, an online bookstore might be a good alternative. If you have someone in your congregation with basic technical and web design skills, it is not difficult to set up and maintain a little online bookstore. Three of the major Internet book retailers—Amazon.com, ChristianBook.com and IndieBound.org—each have its own referral programs that will pay you a small percentage when a customer makes a purchase through your site. Referral income could help fund the church's library or could be used to benefit another ministry in the church or neighborhood.

Chapter four pointed out how church libraries could be an asset to the neighborhood and also how churches can help support work of the public library. Even if a church is devoting time and energy to promoting the work of the local public library, it might consider maintaining at least a modest-sized library of its own. A public library—and especially a smaller one—will not be able to offer many academic works in theology and biblical studies, which tend to be expensive. It can be a rich benefit to a congregation to have access to reference books of this sort. On a completely different note, maintaining a diverse church library can be a tangible reminder to a congregation that it has been called into God's work of reconciling *all* things.

There are a few of us at Englewood Christian Church who keep much of our personal libraries in the church building and make these books available for the congregation to borrow. These collections are not what you would find in most church libraries. They include works of fiction, philosophy, economics, science, the arts, sociology and more. These diverse collections remind us that we are not merely a religious community that does "spiritual" things but simply a community in a broad and holistic sense. Our work spans all of those categories (economics, arts, philosophy, etc.). We are fortunate that we have a church building large enough to hold all these books, but you don't need a huge space to curate a thoughtful and useful collection.

Although bookstores or libraries are the most common ways of making books accessible to a congregation, they are not the only options. The Renew Community in Lansdale, Pennsylvania, a church with a deep commitment to nurturing the practice of reading, is pastored by J. R. Briggs. For each sermon series, the Renew Community recommends several books for its members to read. J. R. and other church leaders choose these books to engage as many people in the congregation as possible, spanning a variety of reading levels and levels of familiarity with Scripture. Copies of these books are kept on display in the foyer. The church even has a line item in its budget for books. It gives copies to members who agree to read and discuss them with one of the church's leaders or with others in the congregation. A budget is a reflection of our priorities, and the Renew Community has clearly demonstrated its commitment to the practice of reading.

CURATING AND RECOMMENDING BOOKS

Another challenge on the journey to becoming a reading congregation is curation. Who gets to recommend books? What tools do we use to identify helpful books? How are recommendations shared? Pastors and other leaders of the church will often be looked to for book recommendations, but they may not be the only curators. Recommendations may come from the church librarian or from other librarians who are members of your church. They may also come from others who simply love books.

A variety of book review publications can suggest relevant new books to read. The *Englewood Review of Books* and *Books and Culture* review books for Christian audiences. The *New York Review of Books*, the *New York Times Book Review*, *Publisher's Weekly* and *Book Forum* are all excellent sources of reviews aimed at general audiences. Your local library is also a good place to learn about excellent new books. It may even have an area in its building or on its website that features books recently added to its collections.

Another key task of curation is maintaining recommended reading lists. Such lists are often topical, containing recommended books and resources on theological or practical themes. Book lovers enjoy listing their favorite books on a certain topic or genre, but for these recommended reading lists to be most beneficial to a congregation, they should be created with input from multiple readers. At Englewood we have many lists of books that have been helpful to us over recent decades, a time of rapid change. Some of these lists are unwritten, existing only in our collective memory. Our challenge now is to get them "on paper," so to speak. One list contains many of the books on ecclesiology that have been most helpful to us. We take our call to be the church, a local community of God's people in our particular place, very seriously. When new people become part of our congregation, our emphasis on ecclesiology is often foreign to them. It is helpful to be able to recommend a book or two for folks to read.

Where will our recommended readings lists be stored? And how will they be distributed? In the twenty-first century, lists will inevitably exist in digital format somewhere, but they don't have to be distributed that way. If your church has a library, perhaps it could own the task of maintaining reading lists. If not, perhaps the pastor or the church office could do so. The challenge is to keep reading lists preserved and updated but also accessible, so that they will be of use to the congregation.

SUSTAINING A READING CULTURE

If we want to build and sustain a reading culture in our churches, we need to teach our kids early about the relevance of reading to our faith. Even before children can read for themselves, we can read to them from books that convey scriptural stories or other important virtues, convictions and practices essential to the Christian faith.

Godly Play is one practice that uses storytelling and play in intentional and thoughtful ways. Using simple figures and toys, a teacher tells Bible stories in a manner that draws children into them and allows them "to gain religious language and to enhance their spiritual experience though wonder and play."[1] The primary goal of Godly Play is to aim "for fluency in the Christian language before adolescence so that children entering this next stage of development have the ability to explore their existential limits and articulate their experiences in community."[2] The prelanguage taught through Godly Play lays a foundation on which language skills and reading can later be built.

Once children are in the early years of elementary school and able to read, we should encourage them to read the biblical text in their Christian education classes. We should also teach them to respect and help other children who struggle with reading. Keen parents and educators will find ways to connect the reading and learning a child does in school with the life of the church. Encourage children to read and discuss novels that engage vital themes of life and faith: books such as Madeleine L'Engle's *A Wrinkle in Time*, Lois Lowry's *The Giver* and C. S. Lewis's Chronicles of Narnia series. Older children can participate in a book club facilitated by an adult, where they gather to read and discuss a novel or another book and think together about how it relates to the Christian faith.

Books are an essential part of the work of educating a church's teens. Teenagers might also have a book club. If teens are not inclined to read a book prior to gathering, they can read it aloud together as part of the discussion. Reading aloud would slow discussion of the book, but as the practice of lectio divina reminds us, that might not necessarily be a bad thing. The main focus of youth programming in many churches is usually entertainment. While it is good and healthy for teens to participate in fun social activities, a church should focus on education and formation, engaging them in the life and work of the church community.

Reading is one important way youth are formed; conversation is equally important, especially authentic conversation that makes teens feel safe to ask hard questions, hear honest answers and express their heartfelt doubts and convictions. Being able to engage authentically in conversation is a crucial facet of belonging to a community, for teens or adults. High schoolers could be invited and encouraged to participate in certain book discussions with adults of the congregation, as appropriate. Reading and authentic conversation are tools to help youth navigate the often-suppressed topics of vocation, marriage, singleness and sexuality that surround the transition from childhood to adulthood. At Englewood Christian Church we recently had a season of reading, reflecting on and discussing topics related to our sexuality. Although these conversations were frank and somewhat contentious, we invited our youth to play an active role in them. We wanted to emphasize to them that sex is not dirty or shameful but a vital part of God's good creation that we should feel safe to talk about.

College students inevitably have their plates full when it comes to reading. However, this a critical time to encourage students to think of reading as a core spiritual practice. One fruitful approach might be to spend time with them, one-on-one or in small groups, and chat with them about what they are reading and studying and how it relates to their faith. One particularly helpful book is *Learning for the Love of God* by Don Opitz and Derek Melleby, which draws connections for college students between faith and their schoolwork.

The work of nurturing a reading culture, like any work done well, is multifaceted and slow. It will unfold differently in diverse church settings. I hope that the many suggestions in this chapter will give you a sense of the lay of the land.

Having explored at length, over the previous chapters, why reading is an essential practice for the flourishing of our churches our neighborhoods and the world, and having offered a few brief thoughts in this chapter on how to cultivate a culture of reading, I pray that you have been inspired to explore reading in a new, deeper and more integrated way in your own church community.

Epilogue

Revive Us Again

The glory of God is man fully alive.

St. Irenaeus

To flourish is to be fully alive. The way of reading that I have described here draws us deeper into the life and flourishing of our churches, our neighborhoods and the world. God created us with an innate curiosity, which fuels our desire to learn and propels us into our calling as disciples. Self-improvement and self-fulfillment, however, are not the primary ends toward which our desires to learn are driving us. Rather, God created us to learn in order to share our wisdom and be drawn into deeper connection with others.

Part of being fully alive is discerning a vocation and maturing in it. Both of these facets of our vocation—as laid out in chapter four—are deeply rooted in the shared life of the church community. In his renowned book *After Virtue*, philosopher Alasdair

MacIntyre describes the dynamics of excelling (that is, being fully alive) within a vocation. Excellence, MacIntyre observes, is seen first of all in the exceptional quality of the fruit of one's labors, a quality that "has to be understood historically."[1] Excelling, by definition, is going beyond. We cannot know that we excel, MacIntyre argues, without a deep sense of the work of those who have preceded us. Consider, for example, a person with no background in art who sees a piece of modern art, say a Jackson Pollock painting, and who thinks, *That is not excellent; I could have done that myself.* But what makes modern art excellent, by MacIntyre's definition, is that it attentively follows in the tradition of previous generations of artists and offers creative responses to problems that arose in the work of these earlier artists.

In addition to the excellence of the fruit of our labors, MacIntyre suggests that a benefit of engaging seriously in a particular sort of work is the rich and meaningful life that it creates. MacIntyre emphasizes that this sort of life and flourishing consists of two essential elements. The first element is improving our skills by doing a particular type of work over and over. The second element is conversation: a dialogue with both the tradition of others who have done this work in the past and peers who are doing similar work now. I would add that regardless of the sort of work being done, reading will play a significant role in understanding and entering into the conversation about the work we are doing.

For disciples of Jesus, our first and primary vocation is to follow in the way of Jesus as part of a church community. Thus there are two primary conversations that we are always navigating between as we seek to flourish, to become fully alive. Not only do we have a community of people who do similar work, as MacIntyre describes; we also are part of a church community that is in conversation with one another and with those who have gone before us in the faith. These local church conversations guide us as we seek to mature in our embodiment of Jesus. They also help us to orchestrate the vocations of our members in a way that bears witness to the reconciling love of Christ. These conversations—with brothers and sisters in Christ and with those who do similar work—are the nutrient-rich soil in which we take root and grow. In conversation we are sustained by the wisdom of those who have gone before us. We are also empowered to discern how we will face the challenges of both the present and the future. Reading is essential to this conversational way of life, as we often cannot literally converse with our forebears or with those who are following similar vocations in other places. We read as a way of listening to the wisdom of others. The conversation continues as we reply to this wisdom both internally and externally. Internally, we reply as we grapple to make sense of this wisdom in our own context. Externally, we reply to our reading as we discuss it with our church or work community.

Finding ourselves in the last days of the modern age, we have inherited a world ripped asunder and smashed to the tiniest of bits. We are starving and gasping for air, cut off from many of the channels that feed and sustain us. Our best hope, it seems, lies in religion (from the Latin root *religare*, meaning "to bind again"), the slow work of binding together things that have been torn apart. The vision of the local church as a learning organization sketched in this book is thus a religious vision: binding together individual Christians in their church communities, church communities in their places, and places in the wondrous whole of creation. Faith and work, being and doing, a rootedness in history and a vision for the future, all brought together with fervent prayer that the Great Healer might continue the work of mending our broken world.

Reading, reflecting, conversing, learning, working, binding together: these are the ways in which our communities—church, neighborhood and world—begin to mature and flourish. This interconnected life is the joyous and meaning-rich end for which we were created. This is humanity fully alive!

In the age of fast food and fast culture, we are often inclined to speed along with the flow of traffic on the highway leading to the death and destruction of creation. Will we, through practices of reading and conversation, attempt to exit from this highway? Will we begin to crawl, perhaps even to take baby steps, along the path that leads to life and flourishing?

Acknowledgments

Although this book bears my name, it—like all books, I suspect—was written in community. Writing acknowledgments is always delightful, as it offers the opportunity to name the community in which the book has taken shape and to remember with gratitude each person's unique contribution.

Above all, thanks to my dear wife, Jeni Newswanger Smith, and our kids, who patiently bore with me in the labor to bring this book to fruition. I am grateful for all the ways that they make space daily for me to do the work I love: reading, writing, reviewing, editing.

Thanks also to Englewood Christian Church for all you have taught me about reading for the common good. This book would have never existed without our life together and our seeking to grow into a more mature expression of Christ's body in our neighborhood. Special thanks to the small group of Englewood brothers and sisters who met regularly with me to read and discuss chapter drafts. Susan Adams, thanks for reading and commenting on the latter chapters of the book in a swift manner as I hurtled toward my final manuscript deadlines. Joe Bowling, thanks for taking the time to talk through chapter eight with me and offering suggestions from your experience.

To my parents, Charlie and Kathy Smith, thank you for not only teaching me to read but also to love reading and to be prepared for a lifetime of reading and learning.

Thank you to Cindy Bunch, my editor at InterVarsity Press. Your thorough scrutiny of my early drafts and your recommended revisions have made this a much more readable book! Thanks also to all the hardworking folks at IVP who have worked (or will work) on this book project.

Thanks to my *Slow Church* coauthor, John Pattison, who meticulously went through an early draft of this book, helping to fine-tune and sharpen my prose. I am deeply indebted to your gift of wordcraft, and to your generosity with it.

Conversations with my friend Todd Edmondson about reading, imagination and the work of Charles Taylor were immensely helpful in the task of writing chapter two. Thank you, Todd!

A deep thanks to all those who participate in the *Englewood Review of Books* community: writing reviews, subscribing to our print magazine, reading online articles. You might not realize it, but you have been collaborators in the ongoing experiment of learning what it might mean to read for the common good.

Thanks to Beth and Dave Booram for their hospitality at the Sustainable Faith Indy house. A large chunk of this book was imagined, written and revised under your roof, and your hospitality continues to be refreshing to my weary soul.

I am indebted to the work of bibliophiles Byron Borger (of Hearts & Minds Books in Dallastown, Pennsylvania) and John Wilson (editor of *Books and Culture*). Your friendship has been essential in imagining the possibility of the *Englewood Review of Books*, and conversations with you never cease to inspire me in this work of cultivating a distinctively Christian practice of reading.

And finally, thank you to the Ekklesia Project for the theological roots from which this book grew and blossomed. Thank you for your support of the *Englewood Review of Books* over the years, for creating a space for us to promote faithful reading, not only at the annual gathering but in a host of other ways as well.

Reading Lists

A book about reading would be incomplete without reading lists. My intent in providing these lists is not to unequivocally name the best books or the essential books on any given topic, but rather to recommend further reading if there is a topic mentioned in this book that you might want to explore in more detail.

These lists are far from exhaustive and will likely be outdated even before this volume arrives at the printer. If you are the sort of voracious reader who is always looking for something to read and who likes to keep up with new books that are being released, I highly recommend looking into the online or quarterly print editions of the *Englewood Review of Books* (*ERB*), of which I am the editor. Part of my intent in writing *Reading for the Common Good* was to articulate the vision of reading broadly for the benefit of flourishing churches and neighbors that has driven the work for the *ERB* for almost a decade now.

Although I initially had grand visions of supplementing this book with a host of varied reading lists, I have in the end limited myself to two lists. The first list is closely linked with the basic argument that I develop over the course of the book and contains books related to key facets of my argument that readers might wish to explore in more detail than I have been able to offer here. The second list is a partial list of books that have been helpful for my church as we seek to share life together. Some of these books we have encouraged as many people in the congregation as possible to read. Others were read together by one or more groups of people, and some of these books were read by only a handful of people, but their ideas have shaped our church community.

I include this second list of books (with annotations) in hopes that perhaps a few of these books will be read by other churches and will speak compellingly into their situations as these books have spoken to us.

LIST 1: RECOMMENDED READING FOR GOING DEEPER

Church Matters

This book is built on the conviction that local church communities play an essential role in the work that God is doing in the world. I don't spend much time here defending this conviction, but here are a few books that do make this case:

- C. Christopher Smith and John Pattison, *Slow Church: Cultivating Community in the Patient Way of Jesus* (IVP Books, 2014)

  Although *Reading for the Common Good* is not strictly a follow-up to this previous book that I coauthored, it does build upon the central conviction of *Slow Church*, that church matters. Chapter one of this earlier book in particular is a detailed but concise exploration of the central role that the people of God play in the scriptural story.

- Gerhard Lohfink, *Jesus and Community* (Fortress, 1984) and *Does God Need the Church? Toward a Theology of the People of God* (Michael Glazier Books, 1999)

These two books by Gerhard Lohfink are without a doubt the best and most thorough explorations of ecclesiology available today. *Jesus and Community* was written first and is shorter and more accessible to the average reader. *Does God Need the Church?* covers similar ground but in much richer detail. The latter book is not so dense as to prohibit reading by an interested layperson but will require a healthy bit of patience and tenacity.

Introduction: The Local Church as Learning Organization

• Peter Senge, *The Fifth Discipline* (Doubleday, 1990)

This is the landmark book that introduced the concept of a learning organization. It is an essential book, but unless you are working in the business environment, the case studies that make up the bulk of the book can be skimmed over. The important contribution of *The Fifth Discipline* is Senge's depiction of what a learning community is and how it works.

• Peter Senge, *The Fifth Discipline Fieldbook* (Doubleday, 1994)

This book, while still focused primarily on the business environment, is a valuable resource in helping organizations with the practicalities of becoming a learning organization. Senge offers much here for churches to consider.

• Isa Aron, *Becoming a Congregation of Learners* (Jewish Lights, 2000)

Although written primarily for congregations in the Jewish tradition, most of the material in this book is relevant for church communities as well, making it the best resource available on congregations as learning communities. The chapters "Text Study as a Vehicle for Change" and "Becoming a Learning Congregation" are particularly relevant to my treatment of reading here.

• Jean Le Clercq, *The Love of Learning and the Desire for God* (Fordham University Press, 1982)

This is a classic book on the practice of study among medieval monastics. In some sense it offers a historical case study depicting the medieval monasteries as learning organizations (although it doesn't use that specific term). Churches today have much to learn from the monastics in their dual focus on reading/learning and on actively embodying their faith in Christ.

Chapter 1: Slow Reading in Accelerating Times

• David Mikics, *Slow Reading in a Hurried Age* (Harvard University Press, 2013)

Despite its release from an academic press, this book is very accessible and the best book available to date on Slow Reading. Although Mikics doesn't focus enough on the social components of Slow Reading, he does a thorough job of helping readers learn how to slow down.

• Isabel Hofmeyr, *Gandhi's Printing Press: Experiments in Slow Reading* (Harvard University Press, 2013)

Hofmeyr narrates the story of the printing business run by Gandhi in South Africa around the turn of the twentieth century and how it was a tool used to promote the practice of slow and attentive reading among the expat Indian community. Although a little more difficult read than Mikics's book, this work does capture the social dynamics of Slow Reading in rich historical detail. It also offers insight into Gandhi's time in South Africa, a little-known era of history for most Americans.

• Michael Casey, *Sacred Reading: The Ancient Art of Lectio Divina* (Triumph Books, 1996)

One of the best books available on the practice of lectio divina, written by a Trappist monk who is intimately familiar with lectio in his daily life. Casey instructs nonmonastic readers in how to do lectio divina, but this is not a how-to book that teaches only technique. Along the way, Casey provides a vibrant historical and theological backdrop for this way of slow reading.

• Eugene Peterson, *Eat This Book: A Conversation in the Art of Spiritual Reading* (Eerdmans, 2009)

  Peterson, the well-known pastor and creator of *The Message* Bible paraphrase, offers a compelling book on reading in the Christian tradition. The section on lectio divina at the heart of the book is a superb introduction to the practice, but I highly recommend reading the full book.

• Carl Honoré, *In Praise of Slowness* (Harper, 2004)

  An extraordinary book that makes a compelling case for slowness in a fast-moving world. Although Honoré addresses reading briefly toward the end of the book, the significance of this book is that it provides a cultural and philosophical backdrop for Slow Reading, Slow Food and other Slow movements.

Chapter 2: Shaping the Social Imagination

• Charles Taylor, *Modern Social Imaginaries* (Duke University Press, 2003)

  This work by Canadian philosopher Charles Taylor provided the basic concepts at the root of my depiction of the social imagination. This book is dense, and reading it won't be of benefit to everyone, but it is immensely helpful in providing an account of how we imagine and act within the world.

• Walter Brueggemann, *The Prophetic Imagination*, 2nd ed. (Fortress, 2001)

  In one of my favorite theological books, Brueggemann explains how the imagination of the Old Testament prophets was essential to guiding the people of God in the ways that God desired. This sort of prophetic imagination is relevant today in navigating social change as we become deeper and more faithful embodiments of the way of Jesus.

• Willie James Jennings, *The Christian Imagination: Theology and the Origins of Race* (Yale University Press, 2010)

In one of the most important theological books of its decade, Jennings explores how the Christian social imagination was deeply corrupted in the early modern era, as Europeans were no longer identified by their places. This displacement led not only to the displacement of native peoples in Africa and the Americas in the colonial era but also to a host of racial, ecological and economic injustices. Jennings's work here is a poignant reminder that we need to be attentive to the ways we imagine the world and how that shapes our theology.

• Eric Jacobsen, *The Space Between: A Christian Engagement with the Built Environment* (Baker Academic, 2012)

A particularly helpful exploration of the ways in which the built environment shapes our imagination and the theological implications of these realities. *The Space Between* is a useful guide as churches seek to reimagine the built environment of their neighborhoods to better promote health and flourishing.

Chapter 3: Reading and Our Congregational Identity

• Stephen Fowl and Gregory Jones, *Reading in Communion* (Eerdmans, 1991)

This book was explored in detail in chapter three; here it suffices to say that it is one of the most important books on Scripture reading in the life of the local church. *Reading in Communion* is the book if you want to deepen your congregation's engagement with the biblical text.

- Philip Kenneson, *Life on the Vine: Cultivating the Fruit of the Spirit in Christian Community* (InterVarsity Press, 2003)

  This is perhaps the best-kept secret among books on church life. Kenneson works through the fruits of the Spirit, identifying ways in which Western culture inhibits their cultivation and pointing us in the direction of a vibrant church life that bears these fruits. Although profoundly rooted in theology and cultural exegesis, this is one of the best practical books on cultivating church communities that flourish.

- Robert Banks, *Paul's Idea of Community: The Early House Churches in Their Cultural Setting* (Baker Academic, 1994)

  This insightful work carefully examines Paul's epistles, with an eye toward understanding the sort of ecclesiology that he was teaching. Central to Banks's argument is the idea that local congregations play a vital role in the reconciling work of God and that a local church is, in a real sense, the embodiment of Christ in its particular place. Both of these convictions are essential to the argument that I make in *Reading for the Common Good*.

- C. Christopher Smith, *The Virtue of Dialogue: Conversation as a Hopeful Practice of Church Communities* (Englewood Review of Books, 2012)

  The Virtue of Dialogue tells the story of my church's experiences with the practice of conversation—how we have been transformed by dialogue and how this practice has been transformative in our neighborhood as well. The book's final chapter makes the case that conversation is vital for the flourishing of our churches and neighborhoods.

Chapter 4: Discerning Our Call

- Luther Snow, *The Power of Asset-Mapping: How Your Congregation Can Act on Its Gifts* (Alban, 2004)

This is a helpful book for churches wanting to imagine in new ways the resources that are available to them in their members and in their neighbors. Although a deeply practical book, this volume shows us what a theology of gratitude looks like— gratitude for all the wonderful gifts that God has made available to us, if we would only uncover them.

• Amy Sherman, *Kingdom Calling: Vocational Stewardship for the Common Good* (InterVarsity Press, 2011)

This is one of the best books on Christian vocation, particularly on the practicalities of vocation in the context of the local church community. The idea of the local church orchestrating the gifts and skills of its members was inspired by Amy Sherman's book.

• Steven Garber, *Visions of Vocation: Common Grace for the Common Good* (InterVarsity Press, 2014)

Another excellent book on vocation. At the heart of this work is the idea that "vocation is when we come to know the world in all its joy and pain and still love it. Vocation is following our calling to seek the welfare of the world we live in. And in helping the world to flourish, strangely, mysteriously, we find that we flourish too." Indeed, if we desire flourishing churches and a flourishing world, we will pay attention to our vocation as churches and individuals.

• Mark Lau Branson, *Memories, Hopes and Conversations: Appreciative Inquiry and Congregational Change* (Alban, 2004)

Mark Lau Branson offers us a practical guide to appreciative inquiry (AI) for church communities. AI is a conversational method that uses positive experiences in the history of an organization to energize it in the face of future challenges. AI is particularly useful for congregations as they seek to discern their unique vocation(s) as a church.

Chapter 5: Reading with Our Neighbors

- Thomas Cahill, *How the Irish Saved Civilization* (Nan A. Talese / Knopf Doubleday, 1995)

  I include this book not only because it tells a story of Christian faithfulness from an era that is little known to most North American Christians today. The story it tells also revolves around practices of literacy and the church's diligence in sharing the gift of literacy with its neighbors, which makes it highly relevant to this book.

- Dwight Friesen, Tim Soerens and Paul Sparks, *The New Parish: How Neighborhood Churches Are Transforming Mission, Discipleship and Community* (InterVarsity Press, 2014)

  No other book makes the case so well for churches as the transformative presence of Christ in their neighborhoods. Amid the present shifts toward local engagement and local economies, the authors of *The New Parish* demonstrate that churches can lead—and are leading—the way in this resurgence of the local.

- Wayne Wiegand, *Part of Our Lives: A People's History of the American Public Library* (Oxford University Press, 2015)

  Wiegand offers a splendid grassroots history of the vital and transformative role that libraries have played in American neighborhoods. *Part of Our Lives* "paints a clear and engaging picture of Americans who value libraries not only as civic institutions, but also as public places that promote and maintain community."

Chapter 6: Deepening Our Roots in Our Neighborhoods

- Jay Walljasper, ed., *All That We Share: A Field Guide to the Commons* (New Press, 2010)

  This inspiring and highly accessible book makes a provocative case for the flourishing of the commons in the twenty-first century. Consisting of a wide range of short pieces by noted writers and activists, *All That We Share* serves as both an introduction to the commons and a call to broaden and deepen the range of resources that we share in common.

• Andrew Dannenberg, Howard Jackson and Richard Frumkin, eds., *Making Healthy Places: Designing and Building for Health, Well-Being, and Sustainability* (Island, 2011)

If *shalom* is the epitome of health and flourishing, then this immensely practical book will point us in that direction. I can think of nothing better for churches to do than to immerse themselves wholly in the work that this book describes, from using the gifts and skills of their members to work in these directions to training up youth to participate in this work to energizing and organizing neighbors to join in it.

• Peter Block and John McKnight, *The Abundant Community: Awakening the Power of Families and Neighborhoods* (Berrett-Koehler, 2010)

The Abundant Community is a wonderful resource on deepening the life of our neighborhoods. The authors describe their aims, which resonate with what I have undertaken in *Reading for the Common Good*: "This book gives voice to our ideal of a beloved community. It reminds us of our power to create a hope-filled life. It assures us that when we join together with our neighbors we are the architects of the future where we want to live."

• Bill McKibben, *Deep Economy: The Wealth of Communities and the Durable Future* (Holt, 2007)

Deep Economy is likely the best introduction to local economies and why they matter in the twenty-first century. McKibben's audacious vision is of "cities, suburbs, and regions producing more of their own food, generating more of their own energy, and even creating more of their own culture and entertainment."

Chapter 7: Hope for Our Interconnected Creation

- Wendell Berry, *This Day: Collected and New Sabbath Poems* (Counterpoint, 2013)

  Poets likely have a deeper sense of the interconnectedness of creation than most of us, and few poets are keener in this way than Wendell Berry. *This Day* is the supreme collection of his poems, and it is rife with themes of our deep entanglement with the whole of creation.

- Howard Snyder with Joel Scandrett, *Salvation Means Creation Healed: The Ecology of Sin and Grace* (Cascade Books, 2011)

  In this book Howard Snyder expands our notions of what salvation is, and does so within the context of God's interconnected creation. Snyder offers us a profoundly ecological vision of the salvation toward which our daily Christian faithfulness should be moving us.

- "Watershed Discipleship," special issue of *Missio Dei: A Journal of Missional Theology and Praxis* 5, no. 2 (August 2014)

  This journal issue is the most extensive work published to date on watershed discipleship; it contains papers by Ched Myers and others.

- Ragan Sutterfield, *Cultivating Reality: How the Soil Might Save Us* (Cascade Books, 2013)

  This is a rewarding theological meditation on our reliance upon and connectedness with the soil. An increasing mindfulness of our connections with the soil, Sutterfield argues, will help us to flourish as individuals and communities.

Chapter 8: Toward Faithful Engagement in Economics and Politics

• Flannery O'Connor, "The Fiction Writer and His Country," in *Mystery and Manners: Essays* (Farrar, Straus and Giroux, 1969)

Although O'Connor is explicitly addressing fiction writers in this essay, I think that it holds profound social and political wisdom for all Christians about the ways in which we bear witness to the gospel of Jesus in the public square. She argues that our faith will foster in us an acute sense of the unacceptable, and that will drive our politics more than a cohesive vision of what the flourishing society should look like.

• Stanley Hauerwas, "The Ecclesial Difference," part 3 of *War and the American Difference* (Baker Academic, 2011)

This section, consisting of five chapters, is one of Hauerwas's clearest and most concise accounts of the church as a political community. The fourth of these chapters, titled "A Particular Place," is especially compelling because it specifically locates the church's politics within all the particularities of the context of the local congregation.

• Wendell Berry, *What Matters? Economics for a Renewed Commonwealth* (Counterpoint, 2010)

Although economics is a thread that pervades all of Berry's work, *What Matters?* is a collection of his essays that most directly explore the economics of neighborhoods and the world. Here Berry turns conventional economic wisdom on its head and makes a compelling case for an economy that puts "nature first and consumption last."

• Thomas Prugh, Robert Costanza and Herman Daly, *The Local Politics of Global Sustainability* (Island, 2012)

The authors of this book put forth a vision of global change rooted in communities that decide for themselves the sort of future they want. The aim of the book is to "help enable us to achieve a sustainable world of our choice, rather than one imposed by external forces." Churches, I believe, can play a vital role in cultivating this sort of change.

LIST 2: ENGLEWOOD CHRISTIAN CHURCH READING LIST
These books have been helpful to us in our continuing journey to discern our identity as a local church on the urban Near Eastside of Indianapolis. Not all of these books will be pertinent, or even of interest, to all other churches, but they have been transformative for us, and likely some of them will be helpful for your church.

I have not included annotations for these books but have noted the ones that were annotated in list 1, as well as those that have reviews that are freely available on the *Englewood Review of Books* website.

   * Annotated in list 1 above

   ◊ Review available on *The Englewood Review of Books* website (EnglewoodReview.org)

Theology

- Gerhard Lohfink, *Does God Need the Church? Toward a Theology of the People of God* (Michael Glazier Books, 1999)*
- Gerhard Lohfink, *Jesus and Community* (Fortress, 1982)*
- John Howard Yoder, *Body Politics: Five Practices of the Christian Community Before the Watching World* (Herald Press, 2001)
- Stanley Hauerwas and Will Willimon, *Resident Aliens: Life in the Christian Colony* (Abingdon Books, 1989)
- Dietrich Bonhoeffer, *The Cost of Discipleship* (Harper Books, 1959)
- Rodney Clapp, *A Peculiar People: The Church as Culture in a Post-Christian Society* (InterVarsity Press, 1996)

- Darrell L. Guder, *The Continuing Conversion of the Church* (Eerdmans, 2000)

- Marva J. Dawn, *Powers, Weakness, and the Tabernacling of God* (Eerdmans, 2001)

- David J. Bosch, *Transforming Mission* (Orbis Books, 1999)

- George R. Hunsberger and Craig Van Gelder, eds., *The Church Between Gospel and Culture* (Eerdmans, 1997)

- Jonathan J. Bonk, *Missions and Money: Affluence as a Western Missionary Problem* (Orbis Books, 2012)

- Christian Mission and Modern Culture Series

  There are many excellent books in this series. Here are a few of the ones that have been most helpful to us:

  o David J. Bosch, *Believing in the Future*

  o Alan J. Roxburgh, *The Missionary Congregation, Leadership and Liminality*

  o J. Andrew Kirk, *The Mission of Theology and Theology as Mission*

  o Philip Kenneson, *Beyond Sectarianism: Re-imagining Church and World*

  o Jonathan Wilson, *Living Faithfully in a Fragmented World*

  o Barry Harvey, *Another City*

- Parker Palmer, *To Know as We Are Known: A Spirituality of Education* (Harper, 1983)

- Lesslie Newbigin, *Proper Confidence: Faith, Doubt and Certainty in Christian Discipleship* (Eerdmans, 1995)

- William A. Dyrness, *The Earth Is God's: A Theology of American Culture* (Orbis Books, 1997)

Christian Community

- Philip Kenneson, *Life on the Vine: Cultivating the Fruit of the Spirit in Christian Community* (InterVarsity Press, 2003)*
- Dietrich Bonhoeffer, *Life Together* (Harper, 1954)
- Arthur G. Gish, *Living in Christian Community* (Herald, 1979)
- David Janzen, *Intentional Christian Community Handbook* (Paraclete, 2012)

Social Criticism

- John McKnight, *The Careless Society: Community and Its Counterfeits* (Basic Books, 1996)
- Wendell Berry, *What Are People For? Essays* (Counterpoint, 1990)
- Alasdair MacIntyre, *After Virtue*, 3rd ed. (Notre Dame University Press, 2007)
- Neil Postman, *Technopoly: The Surrender of Culture to Technology* (Vintage, 1993)
- Neil Postman, *The End of Education* (Vintage, 1996)

Urban Issues

- Jacques Ellul, *The Meaning of the City* (Eerdmans, 1970)
- Jane Jacobs, *The Death and Life of Great American Cities* (Random House, 1961)
- Philip Bess, *Till We Have Built Jerusalem* (ISI Books, 2006)
- David Owen, *Green Metropolis: Why Living Smaller, Living Closer, and Driving Less Are the Keys to Sustainability* (Riverhead, 2009)
- Andres Duany and Jeff Speck, *The Smart Growth Manual* (McGraw-Hill, 2009)
- David Simon and Ed Burns, *The Corner: A Year in the Life of an Inner-City Neighborhood* (Broadway Books, 1998)

Food/Agriculture

- Wendell Berry, *The Unsettling of America: Culture and Agriculture* (SierraClub Books, 1977)
- Michael Pollan, *Omnivore's Dilemma: A Natural History of Four Meals* (Penguin Books, 2006)
- Norman Wirzba, *Food and Faith: A Theology of Eating* (Cambridge University Press, 2007)
- Mary Beth Lind and Cathleen Hockman-Wert, *Simply in Season: A World Community Cookbook* (Herald, 2005)

Poetry

Rather than listing specific books, I will simply offer a few poets whose work has been meaningful to us:

- Wendell Berry
- Liberty Hyde Bailey
- Madeleine L'Engle
- Thomas Merton
- Mary Oliver
- Ernesto Cardenal
- Luci Shaw

Fiction

We haven't read much fiction together as a church, but these are some of the novels that numerous people have read or that have been heralded in the *Englewood Review of Books*:

- Wendell Berry, the Port William Novels (especially *Jayber Crow*)
- Marilynne Robinson, *Gilead: A Novel* (Farrar, Straus and Giroux, 2004)
- Flannery O'Connor, *The Collected Stories* (Farrar, Straus and Giroux, 1971)

- Madeleine L'Engle, *A Wrinkle in Time* (Farrar, Straus and Giroux, 1963)

- Doug Worgul, *Thin, Blue Smoke: A Novel* (Burnside Books, 2012) ◊

Notes

INTRODUCTION

[1]Peter M. Senge, *The Fifth Discipline*, rev. ed. (New York: Doubleday, 2006), 4.

[2]Ibid., 13-14.

[3]Ibid., 218.

[4]Ibid., 10.

[5]Parker J. Palmer. *To Know as We Are Known: Education as Spiritual Journey* (San Francisco: HarperSanFrancisco, 1993), 9.

[6]Thomas Merton, *New Seeds of Contemplation* (New York: New Directions, 1961), 122.

[7]For further explanation of this conviction, see C. Christopher Smith and John Pattison, *Slow Church: Cultivating Community in the Patient Way of Jesus* (Downers Grove, IL: InterVarsity Press, 2014), especially chapter 1, "A Theological Vision for Slow Church."

1 SLOW READING IN ACCELERATING TIMES

[1]Walter Kirn. "The Autumn of the Multitaskers," *Atlantic*, November 2007, www.theatlantic.com/magazine/archive/2007/11/the-autumn-of-the-multitaskers/306342.

[2]Quoted in David Mikics, *Slow Reading in a Hurried Age* (Cambridge, MA: Harvard University Press, 2013), 12.

[3] Mikics, *Slow Reading in a Hurried Age*, 18.

[4]Thomas Merton, *Thoughts in Solitude* (New York: Dell, 1961), 75.

[5]George Ritzer, *The McDonaldization of Society*, 20th anniv. ed. (Thousand Oaks, CA: Sage, 2012).

[6]Carl Honoré, *In Praise of Slowness: Challenging the Cult of Speed* (New York: HarperOne, 2004), 14-15.

[7]Some scholars argue that when he was compiling his famous Rule,

Benedict was drawing on a practice of *lectio* that had been in place long before his time.

[8]Michael Casey, *Sacred Reading: The Ancient Art of Lectio Divina* (Liguori, MO: Liguori Books, 1996), 39.

[9]Eugene W. Peterson, *Eat This Book: A Conversation in the Art of Spiritual Reading* (Grand Rapids: Eerdmans, 2009), 87.

[10]Casey, *Sacred Reading,* 61.

[11]Ibid., 83.

[12]David Steindl-Rast, *Gratefulness: The Heart of Prayer* (New York: Paulist, 1984), 66.

[13]Cornelius Plantinga, *Reading for Preaching* (Grand Rapids: Eerdmans, 2013), 1.

[14]Richard J. Foster, *Celebration of Discipline* (San Francisco: Harper Collins, 1978), 162.

2 Shaping the Social Imagination

[1]Edwin Abbot, *Flatland* (London: Seeley, 1884), 100.

[2]The concept of God's people as a "contrast society" is introduced by Gerhard Lohfink in his book *Jesus and Community: The Social Dimension of Christian Faith* (Minneapolis: Fortress, 1984).

[3]Walter Brueggemann, *The Prophetic Imagination,* 2nd ed. (Minneapolis: Fortress, 2001), 3.

[4]Ludwig Wittgenstein and other modern philosophers have emphasized that our language plays a key role not only in our theories about the world but also in our structures. For instance, in the example of Eucharist versus the Mass versus Communion versus the Lord's Supper, although each of these refers to a similar act, each conveys nuanced differences in how the act is understood and practiced.

[5]Read 1 Corinthians 14:34 in the context of verses 26-40, especially verse 40.

[6]Although Taylor did not coin the term, his 2004 book *Modern Social Imaginaries* was the first work to explore the idea in detail. He continued to refine the concept in his preeminent 2007 book *The Secular Age.* James K. A. Smith's book *How (Not) to Be Secular: Reading Charles Taylor* (Grand Rapids: Eerdmans, 2014) is a superb and helpful introduction to Taylor's work for Christian readers.

[7]Charles Taylor, *Modern Social Imaginaries* (Durham, NC: Duke University Press, 2003), 23.

[8]Ibid., 24.

[9]Charles Taylor, *The Secular Age* (Cambridge, MA: Harvard University Press, 2007), 173-74.

[10]Ibid., 173.

[11]Peter M. Senge, *The Fifth Discipline*, rev. ed. (New York: Doubleday, 2006), 202.

[12]Steven Pinker, *The Better Angels of Our Nature: Why Violence Has Declined* (New York: Penguin, 2012), 175.

[13]Ibid., 175-76.

[14]Ibid., 177.

[15]John O'Donohue, *Beauty: The Invisible Embrace* (New York: Harper Collins, 2004), 12.

[16]Senge, *Fifth Discipline*, 224.

[17]Brueggemann, *Prophetic Imagination*, 21.

[18]I don't believe it is necessary for everyone to read broadly, but I do think it is healthy for the collective range of reading across a local church congregation to be broad.

3 READING AND OUR CONGREGATIONAL IDENTITY

[1]Thomas Merton, *Thoughts in Solitude* (New York: Dell, 1961), 77.

[2]Stephen Fowl and Gregory Jones, *Reading in Communion: Scripture and Ethics in Christian Life* (Grand Rapids: Eerdmans, 1991), 1.

[3]For more on improvisation as a way of faithfully being God's people, see C. Christopher Smith and John Pattison, *Slow Church: Cultivating Community in the Patient Way of Jesus* (Downers Grove, IL: InterVarsity Press, 2014), 22-23; for deeper exploration, see Samuel Wells, *Improvisation: The Drama of Christian Ethics* (Grand Rapids: Brazos, 2004).

[4]Fowl and Jones, *Reading in Communion*, 20.

[5]Ibid., 42.

[6]Ibid., 43.

[7]Ibid., 46.

[8]Jean LeClercq, *The Love of Learning and the Desire for God: A Study of Monastic Culture*, 3rd ed. (New York: Fordham University Press, 1982), 133-34.

4 DISCERNING OUR CALL

[1]Parker Palmer, *Let Your Life Speak* (San Francisco: Jossey-Bass, 1999), 4.

[2]Thomas Merton, *Thoughts in Solitude* (New York: Dell, 1961), 109.

[3]Thomas Merton, *No Man Is an Island* (New York: HBJ Books, 1955), 131.

5 Reading with Our Neighbors

[1]Thomas Cahill, *How the Irish Saved Civilization* (New York: Doubleday, 1995), 148.

[2]Ibid., 163.

[3]Dwight Friesen, Tim Soerens and Paul Sparks, *The New Parish: How Neighborhood Churches Are Transforming Mission, Discipleship and Community* (Downers Grove, IL: InterVarsity Press, 2014), 47.

[4]George Santayana, *The Life of Reason* (repr., New York: Prometheus Books, 1998), 82.

[5]Library website, accessed February 16, 2015: www.whfirstchurch.org/jp -webster-library.

[6]Neil Gaiman. "Why Our Future Depends on Libraries, Reading and Daydreaming," *Guardian*, October 15, 2013, www.theguardian.com/books/2013 /oct/15/neil-gaiman-future-libraries-reading-daydreaming (accessed August 27, 2015).

[7]ProLiteracy, http://www.proliteracy.org/about-us/mission-vision-and -history (accessed February 16, 2015). ProLiteracy is the nonprofit organization that carries on Frank Laubach's mission today.

[8]Connie Claris, "Laubach Has Solution to Problem of Peace," *Times-News* [Hendersonville, NC], September 10, 1968, http://bit.ly/FrankLaubach -NewspaperArticle (accessed February 16, 2015).

[9]Frank Laubach, *Channels of Spiritual Power* (New York: Revell, 1954), 184-85. Italics in original.

[10]Virginia H. Milhouse, *Transcultural Realities: Interdisciplinary Perspectives on Cross-Cultural Relations* (Thousand Oaks, CA: Sage, 2001), 137.

[11]These words, originally written to Madison, have been preserved in an extract that was sent to Uriah Forrest on December 31, 1787. This letter can be read online at founders.archives.gov/documents/Jefferson/01-12-02-0490.

[12]Lee Hamilton, quoted in "Benefits of Civic Learning: Promoting Civic Knowledge, Skills, and Dispositions," National Conference on Citizenship website, September 15, 2011, ncoc.net/Benefits-of-Civic-LearningPromoting -Civic-Knowledge-Skills-and-Dispositions-CMS (accessed February 16, 2015).

6 Deepening Our Roots in Our Neighborhoods

[1]Dwight Friesen, Tim Soerens and Paul Sparks, *The New Parish: How Neighborhood Churches Are Transforming Mission, Discipleship and Community* (Downers Grove, IL: InterVarsity Press, 2014), 112.

[2]Willie James Jennings, "Thinking Theologically About Space: An Interview," by C. Christopher Smith, *Englewood Review of Books* 1, no. 1: 7.

[3]Liberty Hyde Bailey, *The Outlook to Nature* (New York: Macmillan, 1905), 14.

[4]Ibid., 38.

[5]Ibid., 51.

[6]Friesen, Soerens and Sparks, *The New Parish*, 98.

[7]For an in-depth exploration of the connection between abundance and gratitude, see "Third Course: Economy" in *Slow Church: Cultivating Community in the Patient Way of Jesus*.

[8]Ibid., 109.

[9]See, for instance, C. Christopher Smith, *The Virtue of Dialogue: Conversation as a Hopeful Practice of Church Communities* (Denver: Patheos, 2012); Juanita Brown, *The World Café: Shaping Our Futures Through Conversations That Matter* (San Francisco: Berrett-Koehler, 2005); or Sue Annis Hammond and Andrea Mayfield, *The Thin Book of Naming Elephants: How to Surface Undiscussables for Greater Organizational Success* (Bend, OR: Thin Books, 2004).

7 Hope for Our Interconnected Creation

[1]Wendell Berry, "Sabbath Poem 2007, No. VI," in *Leavings: Poems* (San Francisco: Counterpoint, 2009), 89.

[2]Wendell Berry, "It All Turns on Affection," in *It All Turns on Affection* (Berkeley, CA: Counterpoint, 2012), 14.

[3]Ernesto Cardenal, "Nicaraguan Canto," in *Pluriverse: New and Selected Poems* (New York: New Directions, 2009), 130.

[4]Howard A. Snyder with Joel Scandrett, *Salvation Means Creation Healed: The Ecology of Sin and Grace* (Eugene, OR: Cascade Books, 2011), xvi.

[5]Dwight Friesen, Tim Soerens and Paul Sparks, *The New Parish: How Neighborhood Churches Are Transforming Mission, Discipleship and Community* (Downers Grove, IL: InterVarsity Press, 2014), 161-62.

[6]Shalom Mission Communities' website: www.shalommissioncommunities .org/about (accessed April 8, 2015).

[7]Ched Myers, "What Is 'Watershed Discipleship'?," watersheddiscipleship.org.

8 TOWARD FAITHFUL ENGAGEMENT IN ECONOMICS AND POLITICS

[1]Allen Ginsberg, "America," in *Collected Poems 1947-1997* (New York: Harper, 2010), 154.

[2]Clyde Kilby, *Poetry and Life* (New York: Odyssey, 1953), 11.

[3]Flannery O' Connor, "The Fiction Writer and His Country," in *Mystery and Manners: Essays* (New York: FSG Books, 1969), 33.

[4]Noel Castellanos, quoted in C. Christopher Smith, "Not Your Father's Christian Community Development," *Christianity Today*, February 20, 2013, www.christianitytoday.com/thisisourcity/7thcity/not-your-fathers-christian-community-development.html?paging=off.

[5]Ibid.

9 BECOMING A READING CONGREGATION

[1]"What Is Godly Play?," www.godlyplayfoundation.org (accessed August 22, 2015).

[2] Godly Play website information page, www.godlyplayfoundation.org/wp-content/uploads/2014/06/What-is-Godly-Play-Handout.pdf (accessed April 2, 2015).

EPILOGUE: REVIVE US AGAIN

[1]Alasdair MacIntyre, *After Virtue*, 3rd ed. (South Bend, IN: Notre Dame University Press, 2007), 189.

Also by C. Christopher Smith

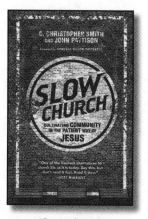

Slow Church
978-0-8308-4114-8

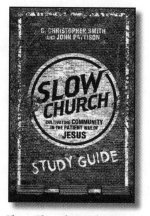

Slow Church Study Guide
978-0-8308-4130-1